Newswriting on Deadline

Newswriting on Deadline

Tony Rogers

Bucks County Community College

PEARSON

Boston   New York   San Francisco
Mexico City   Montreal   Toronto   London   Madrid   Munich   Paris
Hong Kong   Singapore   Tokyo   Cape Town   Sydney

Series Editor: Molly Taylor
Editorial Assistant: Michael Kish
Marketing Manager: Mandee Eckersley
Production Administrator: Marissa Falco
Editorial-Production Service: Colophon
Electronic Composition: Publishers' Design and Production Services, Inc.
Compositon and Prepress Buyer: Linda Cox
Manufacturing Buyer: JoAnne Sweeney
Cover Administrator: Kristina Mose-Libon

For related titles and support materials, visit our online catalog at www.ablongman.com.

Between the time Website information is gathered and then published, it is not unusual for some sites to have closed. Also, the transcription of URLs can result in typographical errors. The publisher would appreciate notification where these errors occur so that they may be corrected in subsequent editions.

Library of Congress Cataloging-in-Publication Data

Rogers, Tony
    Newswriting on deadline / Tony Rogers.
        p.   cm.
    Includes index.
    ISBN 0-205-37798-X (alk. paper)
    1. Journalism—Authorship.   2. Reporters and reporting.   I. Title.
PN4775.R57 2003
808'.06607—dc21
                                                                    2003046377

Printed in the United States of America
10 9 8 7 6 5 4 3 2 1 CIN 07 06 05 04 03

To Minh,
And to my parents

Contents

Preface

From grade school to high school and beyond, most students learn to write in English classes, where they churn out long—and sometimes long-winded—research papers. Deadlines? Typically, students are given weeks to complete such assignments.

Then the college student weaned on this kind of writing happens to take a journalism course. Suddenly, she is asked to write short, tight stories, and to do so not in a few weeks but in a few minutes. It's a shock, to say the least.

But that's what newswriting, and this book, are all about. "Newswriting on Deadline" is designed to give students a crash course in the craft of banging out news stories of all sorts in a matter of minutes. Which, after all, is what 21st century journalism is all about. With cable networks and the Internet making the news cycle faster than ever, reporters at newspapers, broadcast outlets and Web sites must be able to produce clean, clear copy—and do it quickly.

All but a few of the exercises in this book are meant to be done in an hour or less. Many can be completed in 30 minutes or less. Whenever possible, exercises are based on actual stories, press releases or documents.

This book also makes extensive use of the Internet. Some of the newswriting exercises are taken from public domain Web sites, and the Internet Exercises featured at the end of each chapter give students online opportunities to hone their skills.

In the end, however, a simulated exercise is no substitute for hitting the streets and covering actual events. Each chapter concludes with Beyond the Classroom, with ideas for real stories that students can cover.

"Newswriting on Deadline" would not have been possible without the generous help and support of many people. I'd especially like to thank the journalists from around the country who agreed to be interviewed for the book's "Real Reporters" feature. Their insights and stories about their jobs give this book its spark.

I'm very grateful to the Bucks County (Pa.) Courier Times, whose expert photo staff provided many of the book's pictures. Additionally, articles from the Courier Times were the basis for many of the book's newswriting exercises.

I'd be remiss if I didn't thank Melvin Mencher, who taught me when I was a student at Columbia University's Graduate School of Journalism. With his combination of wisdom and curmudgeonly compassion, he's the closest thing I've ever had to a mentor in journalism.

I'd like to acknowledge the following reviewers: Dennis R. Getto, University of Wisconsin–Milwaukee; Julie K. Henderson, University of Wisconsin–Oshkosh; Lil Junas, Wartburg College; Elizabeth Kerlikowske, Kellogg Community College; Judi Linville, University of Missouri–St. Louis; Mead Loop, Ithaca College; and Jane O. Nicholson, Virginia Commonwealth University.

Finally, I'd like to thank my students, particularly those who have worked at the Centurion, the student newspaper at Bucks County Community College. Year after year, their passion and enthusiasm for this profession make me remember why I wanted to be a reporter in the first place.

chapter one

Newswriting on Deadline

*i*t's morning at the Bucks County Courier Times, a local paper in Pennsylvania, and some chatter comes over the police scanner. A dump truck has plowed into several cars, and injured drivers are trapped in their vehicles. The city editor dispatches a reporter to the scene. By the time he gathers the necessary information and races back to the newsroom, he'll have a few hours to bang out the story.

Across the country, a passenger jet bound for Seattle crashes off the Pacific coast. Under difficult circumstances and on a tight deadline, a reporter from the Seattle Post-Intelligencer must write a sensitive feature story evoking the anguish of the relatives who wait for word of their loved ones on the doomed flight.

Move to New York City, where a police reporter for the Daily News, working on little more than a tip, manages to quickly piece together a story about a man and woman who have seemingly vanished into thin air.

And on Sept. 11, 2001, a White House reporter for Cox Newspapers has just a few short hours to turn out a story on the president's response to the worst terror attack in the nation's history.

To the average person, such scenarios may sound like something out of a Hollywood drama. But reporters face such situations daily. Seven days a week, 24 hours a day, reporters for wire services, newspapers, broadcast networks and news Web sites face the prospect of producing well-written news copy on tight deadlines. Sometimes the reporter has a few hours to write a story; sometimes a matter of minutes.

For the aspiring journalist, the challenge of producing well-written articles in less than an hour can seem daunting. Most beginning journalism students are accustomed to English classes, where instructors typically give students weeks to write research papers. No such luxury exists in the newsroom. But newswriting is simply a skill, and like any skill it must be learned, starting with the fundamentals. Just as the piano student learns scales before tackling Rachmaninoff, the journalism student learns how to construct a simple news story before moving on to more complex subjects. Learning to write quickly comes with practice. The more you do it, the faster you'll get.

In this book you'll find a series of newswriting exercises broken down by topic. Each exercise is a collection of facts, quotes and background material. In other words, it's the raw material that the reporter gathers in her notebook before sitting down to write. Many exercises are based on real events, and in some cases, you'll use actual arrest reports or court documents connected to the event. Your job is to take this information and turn it into a news story, and do to so on a tight deadline. Most exercises in this book should be done in less than an hour, many in no more than 30 minutes. You'll find that when you first start writing news, the process will probably be slow. Don't worry. You'll build up speed as you build up skill. Within a few weeks, articles that once took you more than an hour to write will probably take much less time. Again, it's simply a matter of practice.

WHAT MAKES SOMETHING NEWS?

Before we learn *how* to write about the news, it's important to figure out what the news actually *is*. Why are some events newsworthy and others not? How do editors decide which stories go on page 1 of the newspaper, and which get buried inside?

Over the years, editors and scholars have come to agree on roughly a half-dozen criteria that are used to decide whether an event is newsworthy. They are:

Impact

Conflict

Loss of life/destruction

Proximity

Prominence

Timeliness

Novelty

Impact—This refers to the impact an event has on readers. The greater the impact, the bigger the story. Some events can have a great impact on a small scale. For instance, a large fire on Main Street in a small town would be big news for the local paper, but not make the national news. Other events—a war, for instance—could have far-reaching consequences for millions of people and would be news worldwide.

Conflict—This is an element of many news stories. Conflict, whether it is a disagreement at a school board meeting or a riot, is news. Generally, the more conflict found in an event, the more newsworthy it becomes.

Loss of Life/Destruction—Any occurrence involving the unexpected loss of human life or widespread destruction of property is generally news. That's why homicides and building fires, for instance, almost always merit some kind of news coverage, as do natural disasters like tornadoes and hurricanes.

Proximity—The closer an event is to readers, the more important it becomes. A train derailment 1,000 miles away is probably of little interest to readers in your town. But if a train derails five miles away from your community, it becomes very important.

Prominence—This refers to the prominence of the people involved in an event. If an average person is killed in a car crash, chances are it will merit a short story in the local paper. But when Princess Diana was killed in a car crash in Paris, it made headlines worldwide. The more prominent, famous, powerful or important someone is, the more newsworthy he becomes. It's not a very egalitarian way of thinking, but it's the way the news business works.

Timeliness—The news business is all about covering what's happening now, so obviously something that happens today is generally more newsworthy than something that happened yesterday or a week ago.

Of course, some events are so important they continue to make news long after they happen. An obvious example would be the 2001 terrorist attacks. Long after Sept. 11 had passed, reporters continued to write stories about the aftermath and effects of that tragic day. Those stories were timely not because the attacks had just occurred, but because people were still interested in issues connected to what had happened—the war on terrorism, security at airports, and so on. Those issues had relevance to readers long after the initial terror attacks. Timeliness, in other words, relates not just to the actual time an event occurs, but also to its interest and relevance to readers at any given period in history.

Novelty—There's an old saying in the news business: Dog bites man, it's not a story. Man bites dog, that's a story. Anytime something novel or out of the ordinary occurs, chances are it's news. Of course, to some extent all news stories have this element. News, after all, isn't what happens when things go as expected. It's what happens when things take an unexpected turn. It's not news when a jet lands safely at the airport. It's news when that jet crashes on the runway.

Journalists are sometimes accused of focusing on the negatives in life while failing to accentuate the positive. Some journalists have taken this criticism to heart in recent years, and have made a point of writing stories about some of the good things happening in their communities. But like it or not, the news involves what happens when things go wrong. That isn't likely to change. Beginning journalists can use the criteria listed above as a kind of checklist to decide how newsworthy an event is. Generally, the more of these criteria that apply to an event, the more newsworthy it is. Let's return to the example of Sept. 11. How many of these criteria can be applied to what happened that day? On the other hand, how many would apply to the death of Princess Diana? Or to the derailment of a train in your hometown?

Seasoned reporters and editors don't need to look at these criteria to figure out whether an event is news. They have developed, through years of experience, a "news sense" that enables them to instantly ascertain the newsworthiness of any story. As you cover many kinds of news stories and events, you'll find yourself developing this kind of news judgment.

WHAT IS NEWSWRITING?

Now that we've established what makes news, let's focus on writing about it. Newswriting, or news copy, as journalists often call it, is the writing you read in newspapers and Web sites or hear in news broadcasts. It's typically short and to the point, written in a simple, clear style that virtually anyone can understand.

Reporters often call their articles stories, but newswriting is different from traditional storytelling. In a traditional story or novel, the most important event, often called the climax, comes near the end. In newswriting, that's reversed—the most important information comes right at the beginning, or "top," of the story. In fact, the model for newswriting is the inverted pyramid. When reporters talk about news stories, they often refer to the top, middle or bottom of the story. At the top of the inverted pyramid we have the most important, or the "heaviest," information. As we move down through the article, the information presented becomes "lighter"—it's not as heavy or important.

A LITTLE HISTORY

Newswriting of the kind we use today developed during the Civil War. Reporters covering the front lines transmitted their stories back to the home office by telegraph. Sometimes telegraph lines were cut to block those transmissions, so reporters learned to keep their dispatches short and to the point, and to send the most crucial information right at the start.

Because the most important information comes at the top of a news story, it stands to reason that the most important part of a news story is the first paragraph. The first paragraph of a news story is called the lead. In the lead, reporters summarize the story for the reader. News story leads are sometimes referred to as summary leads, hard-news leads, or straight leads.

THE FIVE W'S—AND THE H

But how does a reporter decide what goes into the lead? How does he figure out what the most important points of the story are? Reporters look for the five W's and the H of any story. The "five W's" are the who, what, where, when and why of the story. The "H" is the how. Think of it this way:

WHO is the story about?

WHAT happened?

WHERE did it happen?

WHEN did it happen?

WHY did it happen?

HOW did it happen?

Sometimes you won't have all these elements right away. For instance, the reporter writing an article about a man found murdered on a street corner may not be able to say *why* he was murdered, or even *how* he was murdered. Often, even the police don't know these things right away. Still, the good reporter tries to get as many of the five W's into his lead as possible. And the H.

So, you say, what's so hard about putting the five W's and the H into the first paragraph of your story? Well, there's a catch. Remember that we said newswriting was short and to the point? Well, leads must be especially short. Most editors want leads to be no more than 35 to 40 words long. Many editors insist they be 25 words or less, or just about the length of the sentence you're reading right now. Editors prefer short leads because they know that readers don't have a lot of time. Readers want to be able to get the main point of the story quickly. Long, drawn-out leads turn readers off. Tight, catchy leads make readers want to read more.

So the goal is to write a lead for what can often be a complicated set of events, and to do it in as few words as possible. The trick? Remember, the lead is a summary of the story. It's the story in a nutshell. That means we only need to include the most important information. The secondary details should be left out of the lead. They go somewhere "down" in the story (remember the inverted pyramid). Secondary details usually include things like exact times, street addresses, and the names and ages of those involved (unless they are well-known).

One way of thinking about the lead is to imagine you've just called up your friend and are about to tell her about some exciting event. It might go something like this: "Did you hear that City Hall burned down today? Some old wiring sparked the blaze and the mayor barely escaped!" There's your lead. Obviously, you'll word it a little differently, but essentially, what you've just said aloud is the lead. *City Hall burned down. Old wiring in the basement started the fire. The mayor barely escaped.* Those are the main points of the story, and notice that you've naturally worked in the five W's and the H:

WHO was involved—the mayor

WHAT happened—City Hall burned down

WHERE did it happen—obviously, City Hall

WHEN did it happen—today

WHY did it happen—old wiring

HOW did it happen—old wiring in the basement started it

When we speak, particularly when we have important news to convey, we have a natural tendency to get to the point. Remember your phone call with your friend, and you won't go too far wrong.

Reporters try to get the five W's and the H into their leads, but sometimes, one aspect or angle of the story stands out as particularly interesting or important. For instance, when John F. Kennedy Jr. and his wife and her sister were killed in a private plane crash, newspapers didn't write the story this way:

A man, his wife and her sister were killed when their private plane crashed off the Massachusetts coast last night.

Pretty silly, right? What reporters actually wrote went more like this:

John F. Kennedy Jr., his wife and her sister were killed when their private plane crashed off the Massachusetts coast last night.

What's the difference? Obviously, the second lead includes who was killed. It does so because the who in this case was a celebrity—John F. Kennedy Jr. The reporter plays up the *who* of the story because it is particularly newsworthy. Planes crash all the time. But it's not every day that a famous person is killed in a plane crash. The death of a celebrity is what set this story apart.

Sometimes, the *what* is the most newsworthy part of the story. The Sept. 11 terrorist attacks would be a good example. Simply telling readers *what* happened is most important. Other times, the *where* or the *why* of the story may be the most interesting angle. The point is, the good reporter is always looking for one particular angle that makes a story interesting. If that angle exists, the reporter highlights it in his lead.

THE REST OF THE STORY

So you've written your lead. You've summed up the main point of the story in 35 words or less, and you've done it in a way that makes readers want to pore over the rest of the story. What's next?

The rest of your story should *amplify*, *illuminate* and *elaborate on* what the lead says. If your lead says that two people were injured in a car crash, then the rest of the story should fill in the reader on the details of the story. And since we are writing in the inverted pyramid form, the information you present should gradually lessen in importance as you move down into the story.

Like the lead, the rest of your story should be relatively brief. The "news hole," the amount of space newspapers have for news (as opposed to advertising), is always limited, so news stories are generally short. Sentences should be lean, and paragraphs should generally be no more than one or two sentences long. (Short paragraphs look less intimidating to readers, and are easier for editors to trim on a tight deadline.)

SUBJECT-VERB-OBJECT

Reporters try to follow the S-V-O formula for writing. S-V-O stands for Subject-Verb-Object, and it's a simple, straightforward way to keep news copy tight. Here's an example:

She threw the baseball.

She is the subject; *threw* is the verb; the *ball* is the object. Now compare that sentence to this one:

The baseball was thrown by her.

Notice that the second sentence strays from the S-V-O formula. So what's the difference? Well, the first sentence is four words long, the second sentence is six words long. Two additional words may not seem like much, but if you're writing a news story that's say, 60 sentences long, those extra words start to add up. There's no room in newswriting for excess words. Keep it lean, is our motto.

Also, the first sentence is a strong, clear statement. We can almost see someone throwing that baseball. The second sentence, on the other hand, seems somehow pale and weak by comparison. The action of the sentence—the connection between the subject and what she is doing—is diluted. In newswriting we want strong, active sentences that move our story along. In fact, the S-V-O form is what's called an *active* sentence construction. *She threw the baseball* is written in an active voice, while *the baseball was thrown by her* is written in the passive voice. Whenever possible, newswriting should be in the active voice. Active-voice sentences are shorter, more concise, and have more oomph.

GETTING THE FULL STORY

News stories should be succinct and to the point, but they must also be thorough. They should answer the questions posed by the five W's and the H and should provide enough detail so that readers aren't left with any lingering questions. If questions are left unanswered, the reporter should make it clear why they can't yet be answered.

Police said they didn't know why the man was shot, or who shot him. They said the suspect was still at large.

In this case, the police don't yet know who did the shooting or why, so it's understandable that those questions remain a mystery.

Editors have a word for unanswered questions in news stories—a hole. If an editor finds a hole in a story, she's going to want the reporter to go back and gather more information until that hole has been filled.

OBJECTIVITY AND FAIRNESS

News stories must also be objective. That means the reporter doesn't inject his feelings or opinions into the story. He simply tells his readers what happened—"Just the facts, maam," as the detective in the old TV show "Dragnet" used to say. That means news stories must be written in a neutral, impartial tone that betrays no bias or prejudice on the reporter's part. Generally, reporters try to avoid using adjectives or descriptive phrases in a way that might show how they feel about an issue.

The heroic protesters braved a fierce storm to stage their demonstration against the government's unjust policies.

By describing the protesters as "heroic" and the government's policies as "unjust," the reporter has made it clear how he feels about this story. Anyone reading that sentence immediately understands that they aren't getting an impartial account of this protest, but rather a slanted, one-sided view.

Not all journalism is done objectively. Editorial writers and movie critics, for instance, are paid to have strong opinions and to write about them. And in fields like public relations and advertising, writers are employed to convey one point of view or another. But journalists have a singular mission—not to report just one side of an issue, but to convey the truth as best they can. That's why, when it comes to the news section of the paper, objectivity is essential. Readers want to be told *what* happened, not *what they should think* about what happened. Reporters who let their personal opinions seep into their news stories quickly lose their credibility with readers.

Fairness goes hand-in-hand with objectivity. A fair reporter is evenhanded in the way he reports on the people and issues in the news in his community. For instance, let's say the local school board holds a meeting in which area residents discuss whether a new school should be built. Some residents argue that a new school is a waste of money and will raise local tax rates. Others argue just as passionately that a new school is desperately needed to maintain high-quality education for local schoolchildren. The reporter covering this meeting may have strong feelings about the issue. But he doesn't let his own views cloud how he reports this meeting. He gives equal space in his story to both sides of the argument, content to let readers make up their own minds.

THE ASSOCIATED PRESS AND AP STYLE

You may have heard of The Associated Press. You've almost certainly read an Associated Press news story. Every time you see "AP" at the top of a newspaper article, that means it's an Associated Press story. What you may not know is that the AP is the oldest and largest news service in the world.

The AP, or "the wire" as it's sometimes called, was founded in 1848 as a cooperative venture designed to provide news to six large New York newspapers. Today the AP continues its mission of providing news copy to newspapers, but that mission has expanded dramatically. The AP now serves more than 1,500 newspapers and 5,000 broadcast outlets in the United States alone. It has 242 bureaus worldwide that feed up-to-the-minute news, sports, business, weather and more to its subscribers. Most newspapers in the United States subscribe to the AP. For many small and medium-sized local newspapers that can't afford to pay a team of far-flung correspondents, the AP is the primary news source for all state, national and international coverage.

A discussion of the AP is important at this point, because most newspapers follow what's called "AP style." AP style is simply a uniform format for writing things like street addresses, numbers, dollar amounts and dates in news stories. It would look silly to write "5 percent" in a story on page 1, then write "five %" in a story on page 11. AP style provides a standardized format for such things.

You were probably required to buy "The Associated Press Stylebook and Libel Manual" for your newswriting course. The book can look formidable at first, but it's made to be used by editors on tight deadlines and is actually very user-friendly. No one expects you to memorize the stylebook. But since most newspapers observe AP style, it's a good idea to start making your stories conform to this format. Get into the habit of checking the stylebook whenever you're not sure how to write something like a percentage, an official title, or a string of numbers. And as you move forward in your journalism career, hold on to your AP stylebook. You'll use it until the day you retire.

In Appendix A, you'll find a cheat sheet outlining AP style in some of the most commonly used areas. But remember, always refer to your AP stylebook if you're uncertain about how to write something.

A WORD ABOUT THE FORMAT OF THIS BOOK

As mentioned earlier, this book is divided up into chapters that correspond to the typical news beats on a newspaper. A news beat is simply a specific topic or area that a reporter covers, such as the police, courts or the city council. At the start of each chapter you'll find guidelines and tips for writing stories about that particular beat. Then come a series of exercises, which generally start out easy and get harder as you move through the chapter. Then comes the Real Reporter section, which profiles a journalist who has covered that beat. The profile is accompanied by one of the reporter's published stories.

The last two sections of each chapter are called Internet Exercises and Beyond the Classroom. Internet Exercises features a set of hyperlinks to Web sites that can be used for still more newswriting exercises. These links, along with many others, can be found on the Web site that accompanies this book (www.ablongman.com/rogers1e). Beyond the Classroom suggests ways you can get out into your community to cover actual events.

LEARN IT BY DOING IT

While the exercises in this book can be helpful in learning to write clean news copy quickly, there is no substitute for hitting the streets and covering real news events. Newswriting exercises can't convey the complexity, subtlety and excitement of covering a real crime scene, court case or sporting event. If you really want to be a reporter, take every opportunity to cover actual news stories for a real publication. Your school newspaper is an excellent place to start. If your school doesn't have a student newspaper, inquire at your local newspaper about the possibility of doing stories as a freelancer, also called a stringer. Many newspapers also have internships that give journalism students the opportunity to get real-world experience in a professional newsroom environment.

The point is, the best way to learn to be a reporter is by doing what reporters do— covering events and writing about them. Once you've experienced the adrenaline rush of covering your first breaking news story on a tight deadline, once you've seen your byline in print in a real newspaper, you'll truly understand the excitement that comes with being a reporter.

QUICK TIPS ON WRITING HARD NEWS

Here's a quick review of what we've learned:

- Leads should be one sentence, usually no more than 35 to 40 words long.
- The lead should summarize the main point of the story but not be crammed with unnecessary details.

    Bad lead: John L. Doe, 35, of 4753 Elmwood St. in Newtown, was in critical condition at St. Mary's Hospital after he was shot in the head in a fight at Jack's Bar, 3724 Maple St., at 8:25 p.m. last night, said police officer Jim Smith.

    Good lead: A Newtown man was in critical condition after he was shot in the head in a bar fight last night, police said.

- Unnecessary details include names, street addresses, exact times, etc. Put them in the story, but not in the lead.

- Generally, don't put a name in the lead unless you're writing about someone who's very well-known, either nationally, internationally or in your community.
- Sentences should be short and tight.

Bad: All the residents managed to escape in time without being injured.

Good: The residents escaped unhurt.

Bad: It is suspected that drug users were the cause of the blaze.

Good: Drug users may have caused the blaze.

Bad: According to Fire Capt. Bill Jackson, the fire started at about 9:45 and was under control by the fire department within 30 minutes.

Good: Fire Capt. Bill Jackson said the fire started at about 9:45 p.m. It was under control within 30 minutes.

- Paragraphs should be no more than a sentence or two each.
- Use active, not passive verbs.

Bad: He was slugged by the mugger.

Good: The mugger slugged him.

2

Rewriting
Press Releases

*i*t's a classic newsroom scenario—a city editor tosses a press release onto a cub reporter's desk and growls, "Rewrite this!" It's something every reporter has done at some time or another, and it's one of the most basic tasks a reporter can perform. But rewriting a press release requires skill and is an excellent way for the beginning reporter to learn the craft of newswriting.

Reporters generally don't like the idea of simply rewriting a press release. They much prefer to do their own interviews, gather their own information, and write stories based on their own reporting. But sometimes, when deadlines are closing in, time is running short and the editor needs to fill a space in the newspaper, all a reporter can do is rewrite a press release. And there is never a shortage of such releases. Every day, police departments, government agencies, corporations, nonprofit groups and others send out press releases by the hundreds.

WHY REWRITE?

The beginning reporter may wonder why press releases need to be rewritten at all. After all, they've already been written by people who are presumably professionals at what they do. Why not just place them in the paper as is? There are several reasons:

Length   Most press releases are way too long. They say in 1,000 words what a good reporter can say in 250 or less. They almost always need to be tightened—a lot.

Hype   Many press releases, especially those from corporations, are filled with public relations hype and hyperbolic language that simply cannot be used in a straight news story (remember the discussion of objectivity in Chapter 1). Such releases need to be rewritten using the neutral language and phrasing of newswriting.

Jargon   Some press releases are filled with jargon and technical terms that the average reader just doesn't understand. The reporter doing a rewrite job has to simplify the language so that everyone—from the fifth grader to the college professor—can understand what is being discussed.

Buried Leads   Reporters know that the most interesting information in a story should go at the very top, in the lead. But many people who write press releases seem not to have learned this lesson. They often bury the most interesting and important information in the middle of the story. A good reporter moves the good stuff into the lead.

The exercises that follow present a series of press releases from several federal government agencies. Rewrite them in news style and cut them to a specific length. Note the deadline for completing the story. Subsequent chapters follow a similar format.

exercise one

Rewrite this press release from the Bureau of Transportation Statistics. Your rewrite should be no more than 150 words. Deadline: 30 minutes.

Inner-city gasoline service stations are the business sector most likely to suffer from diversion of traffic to highway bypasses in small cities when compared to retail stores, eating and drinking establishments, and service industry locations, according to a new study in "The Journal of Transportation and Statistics" released today by the Bureau of Transportation Statistics (BTS). Retail stores and eating and drinking establishments typically face less negative impacts, according to the article. "The better a relief route works from a traffic standpoint, the greater its adverse impact on per capita local sales," the study found. Service industries, the fourth sector studied, see only minimal impacts.

The study, "The Impacts of Bypasses on Small and Medium-Sized Communities: An Econometric Analysis," examined 42 Texas cities of less than 50,000 population. It was conducted by Sivaramakrishnan Srinivasan and Kara Kockelman of the University of Texas.

exercise two

Rewrite this press release. Your rewrite should be no more than 150 words. Deadline: 30 minutes.

The U.S. Department of Transportation's Bureau of Transportation Statistics (BTS) today released its monthly "Transportation Indicators" report showing that enplanements on international flights by large U.S. carriers decreased by 14 percent in April compared to a year earlier.

The 4.4 million international passengers on U.S. carriers in April were the fewest of any April since 1996. In April 2001, 5.2 million international passengers flew on U.S. carriers.

April was the first month since October that there were fewer international passengers than the previous month. International traffic had increased each month since October, the first full month after the Sept. 11 terrorist attacks.

The number of passengers declined to a 10-year low of 3.1 million in October. More international passengers returned each month, reaching a peak of 4.9 million in March before dropping back to 4.4 million in April.

There were also 16 percent fewer revenue passenger-miles on international flights by large U.S. carriers in April 2002 compared to April of last year.

The BTS "Transportation Indicators" report is a monthly update of critical transportation information that details the impact of transportation on the nation's economy and society.

"Transportation Indicators" provides information on more than 300 trends in the areas of safety, mobility, economic growth, the human and natural environment, and national security. The monthly report, which is available at http://www.bts.gov, provides information to address specific transportation issues and to assist in the effort led by BTS to make transportation information more accurate, reliable and timely. Updated reports will be available on the BTS Web site at the end of every month.

Other trends highlighted in this month's report are:

- There were 10 percent fewer revenue passenger-miles on large domestic air carriers in April than in April 2001. Revenue ton-miles were down by nearly 3 percent.

- There were nearly 11 percent fewer revenue enplanements on domestic airlines in April—just under 46.5 million compared to 52 million in April of last year.

- Preliminary 2001 estimates show carbon dioxide emissions from the transportation sector, which first surpassed industrial sector emissions in 1998, continue to increase—up 3 million metric tons of carbon equivalent or 0.6 percent from 2000. Meanwhile, carbon dioxide emissions from industry continue to drop—down 43 million metric tons of carbon equivalent or 9.2 percent from 2000. Preliminary estimates of carbon dioxide emissions from the commercial sector show a 6 percent increase.

- The underlying trend for highway hazardous materials incidents indicates a decline in incidents after September 2001. Because the 2001 data are still preliminary, the final data may show a change in this decline.

- The underlying trend for public transit ridership shows a decline in ridership since September 2001.

- U.S. international container traffic decreased 32 percent in the first quarter of 2002 compared to the first quarter of 2001, to the lowest level since 1994.

- Motor vehicle insurance costs rose 9 percent in the past year.

- Producer prices for crude petroleum declined 18 percent while producer prices for petroleum products declined 16 percent in June compared to June 2001.

- Producer prices for water transportation increased 4 percent in June over June 2001. The nearly 3 percent increase in producer prices for freight railroad transportation over the 12 months ending in June was the second largest increase for this series in the 10 years tracked by this report.
- Producer prices for passenger rail transportation rose 6 percent in June compared to June 2001.
- Average hourly earnings of water transportation services workers increased 8 percent (in current dollars) in May over May 2001. Earnings have increased 21 percent since May 1999.
- Transportation industry income was up 2 percent, at a seasonally adjusted rate, in the first quarter of 2002 compared to the fourth quarter of 2001. However, when compared with the first quarter of 2001, it was down 7 percent.
- After falling 19 percent from June 2000 to September 2001, manufacturers' new orders rose in May for the third straight month, improving prospects for increased freight business.
- Private investment in transportation equipment declined 7 percent (in current dollars) in the first quarter of 2002 compared to the same quarter last year.

- After falling 7 percent from June 2000 to December 2001, industrial production rose in June for the sixth straight month.
- Production of consumer light trucks rose 4 percent in May.
- Production of aircraft and parts has fallen nearly 30 percent since March 2001. Industrial capacity utilization in the aerospace and other equipment industry has fallen to 60 percent, the lowest level since 1995.
- May fuel costs for scheduled large domestic carriers were 70 cents a gallon, down 8 cents from May 2001.
- Transportation energy consumption declined 3 percent in March compared to March 2001.
- Net petroleum imports declined 6 percent in May compared to May 2001.

Continual updating of information on trends will help in developing forecasts for the future, both within the department and outside. The monthly report will also help transportation decision makers spot changes that might require rapid action. The statistical significance of these statements has not been tested. BTS is testing a statistical monitoring process in order to apply statistical quality control techniques to the "Indicators" data.

exercise three

Rewrite the following press release. Your rewrite should be no more than 150 words. Deadline: 30 minutes.

The U.S. Department of Transportation's Bureau of Transportation Statistics (BTS) today released its monthly "Transportation Indicators" report showing that consumer prices for all types of gasoline fell almost 6 percent between November and December. Dr. Ashish Sen, BTS Director, said, " 'Transportation Indicators' helps us monitor our transportation system and its impact on our economy. BTS will continue to monitor the nation's transportation system through this monthly report."

The BTS "Transportation Indicators" report is a monthly update of critical transportation information that details the impact of transportation on the nation's economy and society.

"Transportation Indicators" provides information on more than 100 trends in the areas of safety, mobility, economic growth, the human and natural environment, and national security. The monthly report, which is available at http://www.bts.gov, provides information to address specific transportation issues and to assist in the effort led by BTS to make transportation information more accurate, reliable and timely. Updated reports will be available on the BTS Web site at the end of every month.

The report also shows that employment in air transportation fell 2 percent between November and December. Since August, 114,000 jobs have been lost in air transportation. Previously, BTS reported that employment in air transportation fell 3.6 percent in November, following a 2.8 percent decline in October. There was also a 2 percent decline in aircraft and parts manufacturing employment between November and December.

Other trends highlighted in this month's report are:

- Tonnage shipped in U.S. inland waterways was nearly 12 percent higher in December than in December 2000.
- Producer prices for crude petroleum in December were 45 percent lower than in December 2000, while producer prices for petroleum products were 36 percent lower. However, world crude oil prices have increased recently—rising 2 percent in the first week of January and another 2 percent the following week.
- Producer prices for highway and street construction declined nearly 4 percent from December 2000 to December 2001—their lowest level in almost 10 years.
- Profits of for-hire transportation industries (establishments providing passenger and freight transportation and related services on a fee basis to the general public or other business enterprises) declined 73 percent in the third quarter of 2001, to less than one-quarter billion dollars (seasonally adjusted).
- Manufacturers' new orders for transportation equipment declined 17 percent between October and November, while total manufacturing new orders declined just 3 percent.
- Production units of domestic light-truck assemblies rose 11 percent in November and 4 percent in December. Production of medium- and heavy-truck assemblies declined 11 percent in November, but increased 10 percent in December. Production of domestic car assemblies increased 5 percent in December.

Continual updating of information on trends will help in developing forecasts for the future, both within the department and outside. The monthly report will also help transportation decision makers spot changes that might require rapid action.

exercise four

Rewrite the following press release. Your rewrite should be no more than 150 words. Deadline: 30 minutes.

The U.S. Department of Transportation's Bureau of Transportation Statistics (BTS) today released its monthly "Transportation Indicators" report showing that airline employment and revenues, as well as air traffic, declined significantly following the Sept. 11, 2001, terrorists attacks.

The December "Indicators" report documents the far-reaching impact of the events of Sept. 11 on the nation's airlines, with declines in passengers, flights, freight, load factors and other measures of performance. Although these indicators show dramatic drops for the month overall, the declines caused by the Sept. 11 terrorist attack only took place in the last two-thirds of the month.

Dr. Ashish Sen, BTS Director, said, " "Transportation Indicators" provides the data to show how the events of Sept. 11 had a major impact on our transportation system. Through this monthly report, we can continue to monitor the nation's transportation system."

According to the report:

- Employment in air transportation fell 3.6 percent in November, following a 2.8 percent decline in October. Employment in transportation services such as tour and travel agencies and forwarding services fell 2.7 percent in November.
- There were nearly 18 percent fewer scheduled flights in October than in October 2000. Of those flights, 85 percent arrived on time, compared to 76 percent in October 2000.
- Large air carriers' operating revenues fell 17 percent in the third quarter compared to the same quarter of 2000, while operating expenses fell by only 1 percent.

Comparisons of this past September to September 2000 found:

- Revenue passenger miles were down 32 percent for domestic and 29 percent for international flights.
- Available seat miles were down 19 percent for domestic and 15 percent for international flights.

- Revenue ton-miles were down 24 percent for domestic and 31 percent for international flights.
- Available ton-miles were down 13 percent for domestic and 21 percent for international flights.
- Passenger load factors were down 10 percent for domestic flights and 13 percent for international flights.
- Aircraft revenue departures were down 21 percent for domestic and 19 percent for international flights.
- Revenue enplanements were down 34 percent for domestic and 27 percent for international flights.

The BTS "Transportation Indicators" report is a monthly update of critical transportation information that details the impact of transportation on the nation's economy and society.

"Transportation Indicators" provides information on more than 100 trends in the areas of safety, mobility, economic growth, the human and natural environment, and national security. The monthly report, which is available at http://www.bts.gov, provides information to address specific transportation issues and to assist in the effort led by BTS to make transportation information more accurate, reliable and timely. Updated reports will be available on the BTS Web site at the end of every month.

Other trends highlighted in this month's report are:

- Producer prices for rail freight transportation fell in November, but were still up more than 3 percent since November 2000, after a sharp rise in October. This was the second highest 12-month increase in the five years of data tracked in "Indicators."
- Producer prices of highway and street construction declined 3 percent in November from November 2000, the largest one-year decline since November 1991.
- Public spending on highway and street construction dropped slightly in October, down 0.65 percent from a recent peak in June.

- Consumer prices for transportation services declined 1.5 percent from October to November.
- Advance retail sales of motor vehicles dropped nearly 13 percent in November, after a sharp rise in October.
- Manufacturers' new orders rose 7 percent in October after falling 6 percent in September.
- Manufacturers' new orders for future delivery of transportation equipment jumped 39 percent in October after falling 6 percent in September.
- Highway vehicle miles traveled rose slightly from August to September but were still down 1 percent or nearly three billion miles from 2000 after a drop in June of this year.
- Railroad accidents/incidents fell to a 10-year low in September—22 percent lower than in September 2000.
- Net petroleum imports fell slightly in October, but remained 4 percent higher than in October 2000.
- Retail gasoline prices dropped 3 percent in the week ending Dec. 17—their lowest level since Feb. 22, 1999.
- Motor vehicle fuel economy rose in 2000 for both passenger cars and light trucks—about 3 percent each over 1999—according to the latest data from the Department of Energy.
- U.S. international trade continued to decline in September—imports were down more than 2 percent and exports were down almost 7 percent from August.
- The value of U.S. truck trade with Canada and Mexico declined 14 percent and 17 percent, respectively, in September compared to the previous year.

Continual updating of information on trends will help in developing forecasts for the future, both within the department and outside. The monthly report will also help transportation decision makers spot changes that might require rapid action.

exercise five

Rewrite the following press release. Your rewrite should be no more than 150 words. Deadline: 30 minutes.

The median age of the U.S. population in 2000 was 35.3 years, the highest it has ever been. The increase in the median age reflects the aging of the baby boomers. However, the 65-and-over population actually increased at a slower rate than the overall population for the first time in the history of the census. Both findings are from a Census 2000 profile, highlighting characteristics of the U.S. population, released today by the Commerce Department's Census Bureau.

"While the median age increased by nearly two-and-a-half years between 1990 and 2000," said Campbell Gibson, a senior Census Bureau demographer, "the growth of the population aged 65-and-over was by far the lowest recorded rate of growth in any decade for this age group."

The median age (meaning half are older and half younger) rose from 32.9 years in 1990 to 35.3 in 2000. The rise reflects a 4 percent decline in numbers among 18- to 34-year-olds and a 28-percent increase in 35- to 64-year-olds.

The most rapid increase in size of any age group in the profile was the 49 percent jump in the population 45 to 54 years old. This increase, to 37.7 million in 2000, was fueled mainly by the entry into this age group of the first of the baby boom generation (those born from 1946 to 1964).

"The slower growth of the population 65 and over," Gibson said, "reflects the relatively low number of people reaching 65 during the past decade because of the relatively low number of births in the late 1920s and early 1930s."

Besides data on age, the U.S. profile contains data on sex, household relationship and household type, housing units, and renters and homeowners. It also includes the first population totals for selected groups of Asian, Native Hawaiian and Other Pacific Islander, and Hispanic or Latino populations.

Other highlights:

■ The number of males (138.1 million) edged closer to the number of females (143.4 million), raising the sex ratio (males per 100 females) from 95.1 in 1990 to 96.3 in 2000.
■ The nation's housing units numbered 115.9 million, an increase of 13.6 million from 1990.
■ The average household size in 2000 was 2.59, down slightly from 2.63 in 1990.
■ Of the 105.5 million occupied housing units in 2000, 69.8 million were occupied by owners and 35.7 million by renters; the homeownership rate increased from 64 percent to 66 percent.
■ The number of nonfamily households rose at twice the rate of family households: 23 percent versus 11 percent.
■ Families maintained by women with no husband present increased three times as fast as married-couple families: 21 percent versus 7 percent. Married-couple families dropped from 55 percent to 52 percent of all households.

The national snapshot, titled Profile of General Demographic Characteristics: 2000, is the first of more than 40,000 one-page profiles for states, counties, cities, towns and townships, as well as tribal areas, Hawaiian homelands and other areas. The table contains nearly 100 data items, plus percentage distributions. A companion table with 1990 data is attached to this new release.

The demographic profiles will be mailed to states on a flow basis starting in May and may be accessed via the Census Bureau's new search-and-retrieval database, American FactFinder http://factfinder.census.gov. The sequence of states expected for release each week is listed on a special Demographic Profile page http://www.census.gov/Press-Release/www/2001/demoprofile.html. Further information on topics covered in the demographic profiles may be obtained in a series, Census 2000 Briefs, to be released during the next few months. In addition, the Census Bureau will send a copy of the profile to the highest elected officials across the nation for their jurisdictions.

INTERNET EXERCISES

If you'd like more experience rewriting press releases, go online. Hundreds of corporations, government agencies and nonprofit groups are constantly churning them out and putting them on the Web.

http://www.fedstats.gov has links to dozens of federal government agencies that produce press releases.

http://www.prnewswire.com produces press releases for the business world.

BEYOND THE CLASSROOM

Instead of simply rewriting a press release, choose one you find interesting and use it as the basis for developing your own story. Develop a list of questions you'd like answered, then call the person or agency that put out the release and arrange to interview them. Write a story based on material gathered from the release and from your own reporting.

3

Police

*t*he police beat is one of the most exciting and important beats on any newspaper. Police reporters, like the officers they write about, often see humanity at its worst—and sometimes at its best. Because the events police reporters cover frequently involve life-and-death stakes, there is no shortage of dramatic stories.

Police coverage involves writing breaking-news stories about the crimes and incidents that police departments handle. Whether it's a bank robbery or the arrest of a corporate bigwig for white-collar crimes, the police reporter must write clearly, concisely and fairly, on a tight deadline.

In addition to breaking news, police reporters write about crime trends in their communities. For instance, is the violent crime rate rising or falling? Why? How is the community affected? And what are the police doing about it? Police reporters also cover the department itself. Is the department doing its job effectively? Is there corruption on the force?

A police reporter's day typically starts at police headquarters, where he scans the arrest log. The arrest log, sometimes called the police blotter, is a daily listing of all the incidents police have handled and arrests they have made in a 12- or 24-hour period. Here's an example (any names used have been changed):

ARREST

Janet Phillips, 31, of Langhorne, Mon, charged with simple assault, harassment, disorderly conduct, possession of controlled substance and possession of drug paraphernalia at Kmart, Lincoln Hwy.

Barn School, Langhorne—Yardley Rd., Mon, 2 female juveniles charged with disorderly conduct after being involved in fight.

CRIMINAL MISCHIEF

Camellia Rd., 10 p.m.–midnight, Sun, pumpkin smashed on side of residence, damaged light pole.

1000 block Old Lincoln Hwy., 11:30 a.m.–noon, Mon, lawn and mailbox damaged, garbage cans knocked over by vehicle.

Toys R Us, Lincoln Hwy., 11:56 a.m., Mon, white male, 6 feet 4 inches, 300 pounds, beard, wearing yellow and black shirt, black jacket, entered bathroom with various Xbox and PlayStation 2 video games, $299.94 value, when confronted suspect threw jacket containing merchandise to floor, fled in 1987 Mercury Grand Marquis operated by female with long brown hair.

Circuit City, Lincoln Hwy., overnight, Sun–Mon, bottom door handle and lock pulled from rear door.

THEFT

Middletown Trace Apts., Trenton Rd., overnight, Sun–Mon, iron plant stand, $20 value.

Kahunaville, Oxford Valley, Nov. 19, backpack from arcade area, contained Sony camcorder, Nextel cell phone, $618 value.

Twin Oak Dr., 10 p.m., Mon, candy cane decoration from lawn.

Reprinted with permission from the Bucks County Courier Times.

As you can see, the log lists quite a few incidents. Depending on the size of the city, a 24-hour arrest log might list dozens or even hundreds of incidents that police have dealt with. Many are relatively minor, while others can be quite serious. Some newspapers, especially small-town papers, publish the contents of the local arrest log each day. But most police reporters don't have the time to write about every minor incident. Most readers wouldn't be interested in such minor matters anyway. So it's the police reporter's job to sort out the small-time crimes from the more newsworthy stuff.

But how does a police reporter decide what's newsworthy? In part, it's a matter of common sense. A murder is obviously more serious—and thus more newsworthy—than a shoplifting arrest. But a police reporter deciding what to write about should also understand the different ways crimes are classified.

FELONIES AND MISDEMEANORS

Crimes are classified under two general categories—felonies and misdemeanors. Felonies are more serious crimes and generally punishable by imprisonment for more than a year. Misdemeanors are less serious and generally punishable by imprisonment for a year or less. Another category, infractions, includes such things as traffic tickets and are not considered crimes. They are punishable by fines.

Felonies fall into two general categories—violent crime and property crime. Violent crime includes murder, rape, robbery and aggravated assault. Property crime includes burglary, larceny-theft and motor vehicle theft.

Obviously, police reporters generally focus on felonies. Most misdemeanors don't merit a separate news story, unless there is some particular angle that makes the story interesting—if the mayor's daughter is arrested for shoplifting, for instance. But police reporters deciding what to cover must also take into account their audience. For example, a bank robbery would probably receive extensive front-page coverage in a small-town newspaper. But in a major metropolis like New York, such an incident would probably end up as a short story buried on an inside page. It's up to the police reporter to decide, based on the seriousness of the crime and the nature of his readership, which stories to cover and which ones to ignore.

Once the police reporter has picked out which stories to cover, he needs to gather more information. The first step is examining the arrest report. The arrest report, sometimes called the incident report, is a more detailed account of the crime or incident involved. The officer or officers at the scene of the crime generally fill it out. Arrest reports can take different forms, depending on the department, but they generally provide basic information—the five W's and the H—on the story. Figure 3-1 is one example of an arrest report.

For the police reporter, arrest reports are an efficient way of getting all the basic facts on an incident quickly. But they are just the first step. Whenever possible, police—preferably the officers at the scene—should be interviewed about the incident. Live interviews provide the reporter with interesting details, colorful quotes and important background information. A good police reporter also talks to people affected by the incident. For instance, if an elderly woman is found murdered in her home, a reporter should try to interviews friends, neighbors and relatives to find out as much as possible about the woman.

PROBLEMS WITH GETTING INFORMATION

Herein lies one of the obstacles often encountered on the police beat—many cops don't like talking to reporters. Sometimes it's simply because they are busy. But more often than not, many officers are suspicious and wary of reporters. Nevertheless, it's the job of the police reporter to cultivate friendly relationships with individual officers on the force—from the police commissioner to the lowest-ranking patrol officer—so that they will be helpful and forthcoming with information.

"It's always good to go out and have a beer with the cops," says J.D. Mullane, who has covered the police beat, among many others, as a reporter for the Bucks County Courier Times in Levittown, Pa. "Cops are an insular group. As soon as you understand that, you can communicate with them better. But sometimes they just won't talk. They clam up."

Beyond one-on-one interviews, some police departments even balk at letting reporters see arrest reports. In these cases, it's important that reporters understand the law. Arrest reports, as long as they don't involve juveniles, are generally a matter of public record and should be available for anyone to see. In fact, state open records laws generally mandate that a wide range of documents produced by government agencies, from the police department to the mayor's office, are open to anyone who wishes to see them. This includes most police records and court documents. But in practice, arrest reports and other pub-

INVESTIGATOR'S REPORT

709 01-11474
Police Offense Number

Prosecutor Case No.

☐ MORE DEFN.

DATE: _____ 11/09/01

CUST	DEFANDANT'S NAME (Last First Middle)	FULL ADDRESS	AGE	SEX	RACE	D.O.B.	STATE & LOCAL I.D.
N	Bleeth, Yasmine Amanda ▓▓▓▓▓▓▓ Ca		33	F	W	06/14/68	N/A

Offense (To be filled in by Prosecutor)

Place of Offense:				
E/B I-94, East of Middlebelt Road, Romulus, Michigan 48174		Date: 9/12/01	Date of Complaint	
		Time: 10:10 PM	11/09/01	
Complainant's Name (Last, First Middle)	Full Address	Age	Sex	Race	Phone No.
▓▓▓▓▓▓	▓▓▓▓▓▓				(734) 941-8400
Person To Sign (Last, First Middle)		Reviewing Attorney and Bar No.		
▓▓▓▓				

GUN USED **N** _____ KILLED/INJURED _____

DETAILS OF INVESTIGATION

SUMMARY:

On September 12, 2001 at 10:10 PM, Officers ▓▓▓▓▓▓▓▓▓▓ of the Romulus Police Department, were dispatched to a single vehicle traffic accident on E/B I-94, East of Middlebelt Road, in the City of Romulus. Investigation at the scene of the accident, revealed that the driver (Yasmine Bleeth) was under the influence of Narcotics, and that she was in possession of cocaine. The defendant (Yasmine Bleeth) was arrested and transported to the Romulus Police Department, where a search warrant was prepared to obtain a blood sample from defendant's person. The results of the blood test, revealed a positive presence of cocaine.

INVESTIGATION:

Officer ▓▓▓▓▓▓▓▓ of the Romulus Police Department were dispatched to a single vehicle accident on E/B I-94, East of Middlebelt Road, in the City of Romulus. The Officers arrived upon the scene of the accident, and observed a 2001 White in color, Chrysler (4door) in the middle of the medium between the East and West bound lanes of I-94. The vehicle was occupied by two (2) individuals, which were identified as Yasmine Bleeth, who was seated in the front drivers seat, and Paul Vincent Cerrito W/M 07/14/70, who was seated in the front passenger seat. Medical personal from CMS Ambulance Unit # 705 were already at the scene, and were in the process of attempting to treat the occupants for possible injuries. The Officers noticed that Yasmine Bleeth was moving around in the driver's seat in a restless manner, and while she was being treated for any possible injuries, Yasmine Bleeth stated to the Officers, that she was under the influence of cocaine, and that she had cocaine in her purse. Yasmine Bleeth further stated that she had been driving the vehicle on E/B I-94, when the front of the vehicle started shaking, at which time she got scared and let go of the steering wheel, and the vehicle ran off the road into the medium. The passenger of the vehicle, identified as Paul Cerrito, also stated that Yasmine Bleeth was driving the vehicle, when the front started shaking and Yasime let go of the wheel, and the vehicle went off the road into the medium of the highway. The Officers recovered the purse belonging to Yasmine Bleeth, which revealed the presence of cocaine.

VEHICLE:

2001 White in color Chrysler four door, Vin Number 2C3HE66G61H655261, Bearing Michigan License Plate UJC129, Registered to Rental Car Finance Corporation (Dollar Rent A Car) 5330 E. 31st Street, Tulsa Oklahoma 74135, with extensive under carriage damage. Vehicle was towed and impounded at J&M Towing, in the City of Romulus.

Detective ▓▓▓▓ # 26	R.M.P.D./S.I.U.	Reviewed & Approved By: ▓▓▓▓▓▓	R.M.P.D./S.I.U.
Officer in Charge Emp. No.	Dept./Precinct/Bureau	Commanding Officer	Dept./Precinct/Bureau

FIGURE 3-1

lic documents are often withheld by police officers or other officials who either ignore open records laws or don't understand them. In one survey, the California First Amendment Coalition, working with the Society for Professional Journalists, found that local California agencies turned down initial requests for records 77 percent of the time. Law enforcement officials were the worst violators, denying a whopping 80 percent of legitimate requests for public records!

In some cases, reporters seeking documents may choose to file a Freedom of Information Act (FOIA) request. The Reporter's Committee for Freedom of the Press—http://www.rcfp.org—provides plenty of information on how to do this. However, FOIA requests are used to get documents from federal government agencies, not local law enforcement officials.

TIPS FOR COVERING THE POLICE BEAT

Attribution

Always attribute the source of your information. In other words, tell readers where the information in your story came from. Police reporters, especially those working the night shift, may not have time to get to the scene of a story. That means they must rely heavily on their sources in the police department for information. If a reporter writes a story about a late-night shooting based solely on information he gets over the phone from the police, it's important that readers understand where the information comes from.

Never Make Assumptions

Never assume anything. Newspaper readers have the luxury of jumping to conclusions about the guilt or innocence of the people they read about, but reporters must stick to the facts.

For instance, let's say John Doe has been found in his house with his dead wife and a smoking gun. Is John Doe the killer? We don't know, and we can't speculate. We can only write what we know firsthand from our own reporting, or what we're told by the police.

Allegations vs. Charges

Reporters on any beat must be absolutely precise in their choice of words, but on the police beat this is especially critical. After all, much of police reporting involves stories about people who may or may not have committed serious crimes.

Let's return to the case of John Doe. If police say John Doe is being questioned in connection with his wife's death, that's what we write. Do we write that he's been charged with the crime? Not until he has been formally arraigned in a court and charged with murder. Let's say the case proceeds and John Doe is charged with murdering his wife. Can we say he committed the crime? Not until he has been convicted in a court. Until then, we must make it clear that the charges against John Doe are allegations, and nothing more. In fact, police reporters often use the word *allege* in stories to make it clear that a person has not been convicted. You might write, *Police allege that John Doe killed his wife*, or, *John Doe allegedly killed his wife*.

Chapter 4, "The Courts," discusses these issues further. But a good rule of thumb for both police and court reporters is this: Never convict someone in print until they've been convicted in court.

Avoid Jargon

Police often like to use what reporters sometimes call "cop speak." It's an absurdly complicated way of describing otherwise straightforward incidents. For instance, a police officer talking to a reporter might say something like, "*The suspect made egress from the domicile and proceeded in a westerly direction. He was apprehended following a foot chase with officers.*" In plain English, please:

> *The suspect fled the house and ran west. Police officers chased him and captured him.*

exercise one

Write a news story based on the police press release in Figure 3-2. Use the Internet to find background information on the person involved. Deadline: 30 minutes.

PALM SPRINGS POLICE DEPARTMENT
Press Release

Type of incident: Drug Arrest

Date: November 25, 2000

Time of incident: 2100 hrs.

Where: 4200 E. Palm Canyon/ Merv Griffin Resort

Who involved (Patrol, Detectives, Outside Agencies):
   Patrol

Why (Radio Call, Search Warrant):
   911 call

Press Release Prepared By (for Media Quotes):
   Sgt. John Booth

Circumstances of Incident:
   Officers responded to an anonymous 911 call, indicating that there were drugs and guns in the hotel room at the above location. Officers arrived and conducted an investigation where we found suspected methamphetamine and cocaine in the hotel room. The sole occupant of the room was Robert Downey Jr. He was arrested without incident.

Arrests (Name, DOB, City of Residence, Bail):
   Robert Downey Jr., 4-4-65, Los Angeles, Bail: $15,000
   He was charged with 11350 H&S (Poss of Cocaine), 11377 H&S (Poss of Meth), 11550 H&S (Under the Infl of Controlled Substance), 12022.1 PC (Commit Felony while out on Bail)

Injuries:
   None

Additional Information:

FIGURE 3-2

exercise two

You're on the graveyard (night) shift at the Centerville Times. You've just checked with cops to see what's going on. Pick the most newsworthy item from these notes and write a story. Deadline: 30 minutes.

11:08 p.m.—Patrol officers arrest man on drunken driving and attempted assault charges. Officers saw man's car, a 1993 Mercury Marquis, weaving and pulled him over at intersection of Norman and Tarrytown Streets. Breathalyzer test showed he had blood alcohol level of 0.21 percent; state level for intoxication is 0.1 percent. When cops ordered the man out of the car he took a swing at one of the officers and had to be restrained. Name is Fred Winters, 28, of 1103 Parkville Lane.

11:29 p.m.—Campus cops called to loud party at Kappa Kappa Omega house at 1234 Gilman St. on Centerville College campus. Officers find crowd of about 50 drunken students outside the house. Loud music blasting from loudspeakers set up on the porch; several students vomiting or urinating on the front lawn.

When cops try to break up the party someone hurls beer bottles from the second-floor window; one officer hit in the head. Drunken students start to surround the squad car, shouting profanities and kicking the vehicle. Injured officer's partner calls for backup. About a dozen squad cars from both the campus police and the Centerville cops arrive. Several students scuffle with police when they try to make arrests. Two students receive minor injuries. The officer hit in the head with a beer bottle, Officer Raymond Santos, suffers a mild concussion; treated at St. Mary's Hospital. Six students arrested and face various charges including assault and disorderly conduct. Takes about 30 minutes to bring things under control.

11:47 p.m.—Police called to 4561 Chancellor St. to check reports of a prowler. Chancellor Street is in the Cornwall Heights neighborhood, where residents have been hit by a series of break-ins in recent weeks. But cops find nothing.

exercise three

Write a news story based on the police press release in Figure 3-3. Use the Internet to gather background information on the person involved. Deadline: 30 minutes.

exercise four

Write a story based on these notes from an interview with Centerville Police Sgt. Wilbur Jansen. Deadline: 30 minutes.

Several squad cars were dispatched to the Burger Boy restaurant, 1125 Gorham Ave., at 12:50 a.m., after getting a 911 call. Turns out two men wearing ski masks entered the place just before closing time at midnight. The two approached the cashier and pulled guns out from under their coats. One gunman ordered everyone to lie face down on the floor, the other ordered the cashier to put all the money from the registers into a bag. Once they got the money the gunmen walked around the place taunting their victims. Jansen

says the suspects put their guns to the back of each person's head and said they were going to shoot. There were six employees and two customers there; all were terrified, thinking they were going to be killed. This went on for about 20 minutes. Finally the gunmen left and drove off. The cashier then dialed 911.

Weapons appeared to be sawed-off shotguns. An undetermined amount of money was taken. No one injured. Suspects described as white males, mid-20s, wearing black or gray trench coats and ski masks. No description of their car.

NEWS $^F_R_O_M$ THE CALIFORNIA HIGHWAY PATROL

PUBLIC AFFAIRS OFFICER LELAND TANG
WEST VALLEY AREA
5825 DE SOTO AVENUE
WOODLAND HILLS, CALIFORNIA 91367
(818) 888-0980
(818) 888-3479 FAX

September 12, 2002

For Immediate Release

Actor Arrested on Suspicion of Driving Under the Influence

Malibu, On September 11th, 2002, @ approximately 12:40 pm., Mr. Nick Nolte was arrested for "Driving Under the Influence." At approximately 12:10 pm, Officer Duplissey, #16657, was completing an enforcement contact on the right shoulder of south bound Pacific Coast Highway south of Kanan Dume Road. The officer heard loud tires squealing from a black Mercedes Benz south of his location. The 1992 black Mercedes Benz was observed weaving across all south bound lanes and into the opposing lanes of traffic. At approximately 12:11 pm., the officer initiated an enforcement stop and the vehicle stopped on the right shoulder on PCH north of Paradise Cove. The officer contacted the driver, who was later identified as Nicholas King Nolte from Malibu, and found the driver displaying objective signs of intoxication. After conducting a field investigation, the officer arrested Mr. Nolte at 12:40 pm. for suspicion of driving under the influence of alcohol and/or drugs. He was transported to the Lost Hills Sheriff's station where he was booked and left in custody.

Questions regarding this press release can be directed to Officer Leland Tang, Public Information Officer for the West Valley CHP, at (818) 888-0980

###

FIGURE 3-3

exercise five

Write a story based on these notes from an interview with Centerville Police Sgt. Wilbur Jansen. Deadline: 40 minutes.

A car crash in Centerville happened at the intersection of Broad and Elm Streets at 10:35 p.m. A car heading north on Broad ran a stop light and hit a car heading west on Elm. Car on Broad had four occupants, all teenagers from Centerville High School. Car on Elm was driven by a 73-year-old woman. Police ID her as Gladys Parker of Centerville. Parker was killed instantly when the carload of teenagers broadsided her car in the middle of the intersection. One of the teenagers in the other car, a passenger in the front seat, was also killed. The other three teenagers, all males, were rushed to Centerville Hospital with injuries. Their names weren't released. The teenager who died was Peter Smith, 17, son of Centerville Mayor John Smith. A number of beer cans were found in the car driven by the teenagers. It's not clear if the teenagers had been drinking or if alcohol was a factor in the crash.

exercise six

It's the day after the car crash described in Exercise Five. Write a story based on these notes from your interview with Centerville Police Lt. Jane Feder. Deadline: 45 minutes.

The other teens in Smith's car were Jim Fogley, 17, Bill Torricelli, 18, and Andy Janko, 16, all students at Centerville High. The three were friends of Peter Smith. All three remain hospitalized in St. Mary's Hospital. Torricelli, the driver, suffered a concussion, bruised ribs and lacerations. He's expected to remain hospitalized a few more days. Fogley and Janko, who were in the back seat, suffered lacerations and bruises and will probably be released today. All three were given blood alcohol tests. Torricelli's BAC was 0.21, Fogley's was 0.18, and Janko's was 0.15. State level for drunkenness is 0.1. Smith's was 0.14. Torricelli will be charged with vehicular manslaughter. Autopsies show Smith died of massive head injuries; Gladys Parker died of massive internal injuries suffered when the cars collided. The teens were at Smith's house before they went out driving; the mayor and his wife were having a party for about 50 guests that evening. Feder says, "Our investigation shows that Peter Smith and his friends were drinking alcohol at this party." Asked whether the mayor knew the teens were drinking at the party, Feder says, "That's under investigation." In a call to the mayor's office for comment, Spokesman George Forrest says only, "The mayor and his wife are in mourning. We have no other comment."

exercise seven

Write a story based on the notes from your interview with Lt. Jack Jones of the Centerville Police Department and further investigation, as described below. Deadline: 40 minutes.

A man walked into Freddy's Liquor Store at 427 Main St. at 7:11 this evening and demanded money from the cashier. Cashier had just $18 in the drawer; the robber got angry, pointed a gun at the cashier's forehead. Cops arrived after the cashier had activated a silent alarm with his foot. Robber realized the cops were outside and took the cashier and two customers hostage.

More than a dozen squad cars and a SWAT team surrounded the store. Police contacted the robber by phone. He demanded a getaway car, and said he would take a hostage with him to keep cops from capturing him. Negotiations continued for about 90 minutes; finally the man hung up on the police negotiator, pointed the gun at his temple and fired, killing himself. No one else was injured. The man is identified as Greg Phillips, age 27, a Centerville resident. He had a criminal record—several burglaries and small-time drug dealing. Jones says Phillips served 18 months in state prison for burglary and was paroled two months ago. He used a stolen .22-caliber pistol in the holdup.

You get the cashier on the phone. Name is Fred Johnson. "I thought I was a goner," John-son says. "That guy had that gun pressed right to my forehead, actually touching it. I thought I was a dead man." Johnson's voice is still shaking from fright. He tells you the two customers taken hostage with him were a husband and wife, and that she was obviously pregnant. Lt. Jones confirms this, but he doesn't have their names.

exercise eight

Write a story based on these notes from an interview with Centerville Police Lt. Mike Kowalski. Deadline: 40 minutes.

Cops raided the home of a Centerville man at 3:35 p.m. today. They found hundreds of pictures and videotapes of child pornography. The material included images on floppy disks the man had downloaded from porno Web sites. Some of the pictures depicted scenes of children having sex with adults. Kowalski tells you: "I've never seen anything like it. There were literally hundreds of these pictures lying all over the house. It really turned my stomach." He says police got a tip from a plumber who was at the house to repair the sump pump. The plumber said he saw some of the pictures in a cardboard box when he was working in the basement. He called police when he got back to his office. That was yesterday. Today police got a search warrant and raided the house. Kowalski doesn't have the plumber's name. But he says the owner of the porn is Harry Johnson, 47, of 2983 Wedgewood Way. Johnson is divorced, lives alone. He's a third-grade teacher at Heywood Elementary School a few miles away. Johnson was arraigned before District Court Judge Jocelyn Malick this afternoon on charges of possession of child pornography and ordered held on $300,000 bail.

exercise nine

Write a story based on the police document in Figure 3-4. Deadline: one hour.

exercise ten

Write a story based on the police documents in Figure 3-5. Deadline: one hour.

| Commonwealth of Pennsylvania | | AFFIDAVIT OF |
| COUNTY OF BUCKS | | PROBABLE CAUSE |

| Docket Number (Issuing Authority): CR-292-02 | Police Incident Number: 28910 | Warrant Control Number: |

PROBABLE CAUSE BELIEF IS BASED UPON THE FOLLOWING FACTS AND CIRCUMSTANCES:

Your Honor, your Affiant is Sergeant Raymond H. Weldie III. I have been a police officer with the Lower Southampton Township Police Department for the past 23 years.

On June 12, 2002, Lower Southampton Police were called to the scene of a shooting at 142 Woodbridge Court South, Langhorne, Lower Southampton Township, Bucks County, PA. Officers Sean Dougherty and Matthew Bowman arrived on the scene at 0236 Hrs. and 0238 hrs. respectively. Officers Bowman and Dougherty found Eric Kassoway, W/M, 19 Yrs., laying on the ground on the south side of his residence at 142 Woodbridge Court South. Kassoway was suffering from wounds to his arm and leg. Kassoway told the officers that he was shot by Daniel STROUSS, W/M, 19 yrs., a known acquaintance, at least two times. Kassoway said that STROUSS fled from the scene in a white Toyota.

Eric Kassoway was transported to St. Mary's Hospital by ambulance.Lower Southampton He was treated by Dr. David Brotman and Dr. Richard Cautilli. The doctors reported that Kassoway was in serious condition. He suffered a gunshot wound to his right wrist and another to his left lower thigh which fractured his femur. Surgery is scheduled later to insert a rod into his leg. Police officers found two spent .380 caliber shell casings and two live .380 caliber rounds on the ground at 142 Woodbridge Court South and on Valley Stream Circle adjacent to the residence.

Northampton Police Officers Trevethan, Budka, and Clifton then went to 144 Cynthia Drive, Richboro, Northampton Township, Bucks County, PA. Witnesses reported that Daniel STROUSS lived with his parents at that address. Officer Trevethan arrived at 144 Cynthia Drive at approximately 0240 Hrs., June 12, 2002 and saw a male outside the residence talking on a cell phone. The male told Officer Trevethan that he was talking to Daniel STROUSS, who was inside the residence at that time. Officer Trevethan retrieved the cell phone from the male and told Daniel STROUSS to come outside. When STROUSS came out, Officer Trevethan took him into custody.

At 0315 Hrs., Mr. Jay STROUSS asked Northampton Police Officer Trevethan if he could speak to his son, Daniel STROUSS. Jay STROUSS spoke to Daniel STROUSS from 0315 to 0317 Hrs., then spoke to his son a second time from 0323 to 0325 Hrs. After the second conversation, Jay STROUSS advised Officers Trevethan, Budka, and Clifton that his kid threw the gun under the deck. Officers Budka and Clifton were pointed to the deck by Mr. STROUSS. They looked under the deck and saw a .380 caliber handgun stashed amongst some wood. The gun appeared to still be loaded with at least one round of ammunition.

On June 12, 2002 at 0905 Hrs., your Affiant executed a search warrant at the STROUSS residence, 144 Cynthia Drive, Richboro, PA. Under the wooden deck at the rear of the residence, your Affiant did recover an Interarms Walther PPK 9mm/.380 handgun displaying serial number S035159. The weapon had one live .380 caliber round in the chamber. PA State Police records show the weapon is owned by Jay R. STROUSS. The same records also show that Daniel STROUSS is not licensed to carry a firearm in the Commonwealth of Pennsylvania.

Based on this information, your Affiant respectfully requests a warrant of arrest for Daniel STROUSS.
CHARGES APPROVED BY BUCKS COUNTY DEPUTY DISTRICT ATTORNEY JENNIFER SCHORN

I, THE AFFIANT, BEING DULY SWORN ACCORDING TO LAW, DEPOSE AND SAY THAT THE FACTS SET FORTH IN THE AFFIDAVIT ARE TRUE AND CORRECT TO THE BEST OF MY KNOWLEDGE, INFORMATION AND BELIEF.

| Affiant Signature | Date 6/12/2002 | Issuing Authority Signature | Date 6/12/02 (SEAL) |
| | Page   of   Pages | | |

AOPC 410B-10-24-98

FIGURE 3-4

INVESTIGATOR'S REPORT

709 01-11474
Police Offense Number

Prosecutor Case No.

☐ MORE DEFN.

DATE: 11/09/01

CUST	DEFANDANT'S NAME (Last First Middle)	FULL ADDRESS	AGE	SEX	RACE	D.O.B.	STATE & LOCAL I.D.
N	Bleeth, Yasmine Amanda	██████████████ Ca	33	F	W	06/14/68	N/A

Offense (To be filled in by Prosecutor)

Place of Offense: E/B I-94, East of Middlebelt Road, Romulus, Michigan 48174	Date: 9/12/01 Time: 10:10 PM	Date of Complaint 11/09/01
Complainant's Name (Last, First Middle) ██████ Full Address ██████	Age Sex Race	Phone No. (734) 941-8400
Person To Sign (Last, First Middle) ██████	Reviewing Attorney and Bar No.	

GUN USED N _____ KILLED/INJURED _____

DETAILS OF INVESTIGATION

SUMMARY:

On September 12, 2001 at 10:10 PM, Officers ██████████ of the Romulus Police Department, were dispatched to a single vehicle traffic accident on E/B I-94, East of Middlebelt Road, in the City of Romulus. Investigation at the scene of the accident, revealed that the driver (Yasmine Bleeth) was under the influence of Narcotics, and that she was in possession of cocaine. The defendant (Yasmine Bleeth) was arrested and transported to the Romulus Police Department, where a search warrant was prepared to obtain a blood sample from defendant's person. The results of the blood test, revealed a positive presence of cocaine.

INVESTIGATION:

Officer ██████████ of the Romulus Police Department were dispatched to a single vehicle accident on E/B I-94, East of Middlebelt Road, in the City of Romulus. The Officers arrived upon the scene of the accident, and observed a 2001 White in color, Chrysler (4door) in the middle of the medium between the East and West bound lanes of I-94. The vehicle was occupied by two (2) individuals, which were identified as Yasmine Bleeth, who was seated in the front drivers seat, and Paul Vincent Cerrito W/M 07/14/70, who was seated in the front passenger seat. Medical personal from CMS Ambulance Unit # 705 were already at the scene, and were in the process of attempting to treat the occupants for possible injuries. The Officers noticed that Yasmine Bleeth was moving around in the driver's seat in a restless manner, and while she was being treated for any possible injuries, Yasmine Bleeth stated to the Officers, that she was under the influence of cocaine, and that she had cocaine in her purse. Yasmine Bleeth further stated that she had been driving the vehicle on E/B I-94, when the front of the vehicle started shaking, at which time she got scared and let go of the steering wheel, and the vehicle ran off the road into the medium. The passenger of the vehicle, identified as Paul Cerrito, also stated that Yasmine Bleeth was driving the vehicle, when the front started shaking and Yasime let go of the wheel, and the vehicle went off the road into the medium of the highway. The Officers recovered the purse belonging to Yasmine Bleeth, which revealed the presence of cocaine.

VEHICLE:

2001 White in color Chrysler four door, Vin Number 2C3HE66G61H655261, Bearing Michigan License Plate UJC129, Registered to Rental Car Finance Corporation (Dollar Rent A Car) 5330 E. 31st Street, Tulsa Oklahoma 74135, with extensive under carriage damage. Vehicle was towed and impounded at J&M Towing, in the City of Romulus.

Detective ██████ # 26	R.M.P.D./S.I.U.	Reviewed & Approved By: ██████	R.M.P.D./S.I.U.
Officer in Charge Emp. No.	Dept./Precinct/Bureau	Commanding Officer	Dept./Precinct/Bureau

FIGURE 3-5

(continued)

REQUEST FOR WARRANT RECOMMENDATION

Name of Defendant #1 Only: Bleeth, Yasmine Amanda ~~...~~   Offense No.   709 01-11474

DETAILS OF INVESTIGATION (Continued)

SIGNS OF INFLUENCE:

Yasmine Bleeth's eyes were dilated and her nostrils were red and draining. Bleeth stated to the Officers, that she was under the influence of cocaine prior to driving the vehicle. The Officers requested her to step out of the vehicle after she was checked by medical personal for possible injuries. The Officers requested that Bleeth perform several sobriety test. Bleeth stated to the Officers that she had no physical defects, including sight and balance. Bleeth removed her shoes, prior to taking sobriety tests on level pavement.

SOBRIETY TESTS:

One leg stand, Bleeth failed to perform this test as shown. Bleeth raised her left foot and tucked it up behind her instead of raising it out in front of her as asked. Finger Dexterity, Bleeth failed to perform this test as shown. Bleeth counted forward then backward on her fingers once instead of doing it twice as asked. Alphabet Recital, Bleeth stated her recital of the alphabet in a fast/slurred manner.

ARREST:

Yasmine Bleeth was arrested for Possession of cocaine, and OUID, Bleeth was transported to the Romulus Police Department, where she was prossessed and lodged without incident. Officer ▇▇▇▇ her chemical test rights from DI-93 form. Bleeth stated that she understood, and refused the blood test she was offered.

SEARCH WARRANT:

Officer ▇▇ prepared a search warrant to obtain blood from Bleeth's person. The search warrant was approved by Assistant Wayne County Prosecuting Attorney ▇▇▇▇▇▇, and signed by Honorable Judge ▇▇▇▇ of the 34th District Court, Romulus Michigan. Yasmine Bleeth was transported to Annapolis Hospital in Wayne Michigan, where RN ▇▇▇▇ withdrew sample of blood (20 CC's) from the person of Bleeth, on September 13, 2001 at 1:05 am.

EVIDENCE:

Item # 1   One (1) brown/gold figured "Louis Vuitton" purse, with white powder residue, containing the following items of evidence.
Item # 2   One (1) Twenty dollar bill, in U.S.Currency, containing a white powder residue.
Item # 3   One (1) plastic bag corner, containing a white powder residue.
Item # 4   One (1) small brown plastic "Vital Express" bottle with plastic top, containing a white powder.
Item # 5   Small plastic case, containing four (4) "B-D" Syringes, containing a liquid, suspected to contain cocaine.

FIELD TEST:

On September 13, 2001 Detective ▇▇▇▇ of the Romulus Police Department (SIU) performed a narcotics field test on a portion of the liquid found in the four (4) Syringes, described as evidence item # 5. The test showed positive for the presence of cocaine.

FIGURE 3-5   (continued)   *(continued)*

REQUEST FOR WARRANT RECOMMENDATION

Name of Defendant #1 Only: Bleeth, Yasmine Amanda ~~~~ ~~ ~~~~~~~ ~~~

~~~ ~~~~~~~ ~~   Offense No.   709 01-11474

DETAILS OF INVESTIGATION (Continued)

MICHIGAN STATE POLICE LABORATORY RESULTS (Northville):

On September 13, 2001, Evidence item # 1 thru # 5 were submitted to the Michigan State Police Laboratory in Northville Michigan, for Chemical analysis. Items 1# thru #4 were accepted, but item # 5 was not accepted, due to being a bio hazard. Item # 5 (Contents), was resubmitted to the Michigan State Police Laboratory in Northville on September 18, 2001, when the contents of the Syringes (Liquid) was submitted in a evidence bottle.

On September 17, 2001 the chemical analysis on evidence item # 1, described as a brown and gold "Louis Vuitton" purse, containing a white powder was completed by Forensic Scientist ▇▇▇▇▇▇. The powder found inside the purse, contained cocaine, which is listed as a controlled substance in Schedule 2 of the Public Health Code of 1978. Weight for analysis 0.013 grams, Weight after analysis 0.010 grams.

On September 20, 2001 the chemical analysis of evidence item # 2 and # 3, described as a U.S. Twenty dollar bill, and a clear plastic bag corner was completed by Forensic Scientist ▇▇▇▇▇▇. The white powder residue found on the Twenty dollar bill and the plastic bag corner, contained cocaine.

On September 24, 2001 the chemical analysis of evidence item # 5 (Contents), described as a clear liquid, was completed by Forensic Scientist ▇▇▇▇▇▇. The liquid contained cocaine.

On September 26, 2001 the chemical analysis of evidence item # 4, described as a small brown plastic "Vital Express" bottle with plastic top, containing a white powder, was completed by Forensic Scientist ▇▇▇▇▇▇ The powder contained cocaine, which is listed as a controlled substance in Schedule 2 of the Public Health Code of 1978. Weight before analysis 0.006 grams, Weight after analysis 0.004 grams.

MICHIGAN STATE POLICE LABORATORY RESULTS (Lansing):

On September 17, 2001 the blood sample removed from the person of Yasmine Bleeth was received by the Michigan State Police Laboratory in Lansing Michigan (Toxicology Unit). On September 18, 2001 Forensic Scientist ▇▇▇▇▇▇ examination of the blood sample revealed 0.00 grams alcohol per 100 milliliters of blood. A preliminary test of the blood revealed the presence of cocaine.

On October 31, 2001 the analysis of the blood sample was completed by Forensic Scientist ▇▇▇▇▇▇ of the Michigan State Police Forensic Science Division (Lansing Michigan). Drugs detected: Cocaine, and three cocaine metabolites.

WITNESS LIST:

Officer ▇▇▇▇ f the Romulus Police Department, will testify to the Traffic Accident Investigation, Descovery of the evidence, Sobriety tests, and arrest of Yasmine Bleeth for OUID and Possession of Cocaine. Officer ▇▇▇ will also testify to preparing the Search Warrant to obtain a blood sample from the Defendant Bleeth.

Officer ▇▇▇▇ of the Romulus Police Department, will testify to the Traffic Accident Investigation and the arrest of Yasmine Bleeth for OUID and Possession of Cocaine.

RN ▇▇▇▇ of Annapolis Hospital in Wayne Michigan, will testify to the removal of 20 cc's of blood from the Defendant Yasmine Bleeth.

FIGURE 3-5   (continued)

Real
REPORTER: Mike Claffey

It's called "the shack." It's the cramped, messy office at police headquarters in New York City where the Big Apple's cop reporters ply their trade. Mike Claffey, a reporter for the New York Daily News, was working the beat there one night when a call came in from a man named Chuck DeLaney. "He said he had a story for me," Claffey recalls. "He said his neighbors had disappeared."

DeLaney told Claffey that his neighbors, Michael Sullivan and Camden Sylvia, had vanished six days earlier while jogging in their lower Manhattan neighborhood. Even though the couple weren't the types to skip town without a word, the police didn't seem to be taking the case too seriously, DeLaney complained.

Claffey was wary. Missing persons reports are all-too common, especially in big cities. Police departments can't fully investigate every case, and newspaper editors are leery of running stories unless there is evidence of a kidnapping, or a child is involved.

But something about this case got Claffey's attention. A stable couple, both with good jobs, had vanished without a trace while jogging. The only things missing from their apartment were their running shoes and a set of keys. A search of the apartment turned up a video rented the afternoon of their disappearance, fresh flowers on a table and new food in the fridge. "This started to rise above the level of a typical missing persons call," Claffey says. "My mind was whirring. I was thinking, maybe this is a story."

Claffey called the night city editor at the News' headquarters in midtown Manhattan and described the story. The editor gave him the go-ahead to write a 10- to 12-column-inch article. Claffey then called the NYPD to get more information, and made arrangements to have a News photographer meet DeLaney to get a photograph of the couple.

By the time he had finished his reporting, Claffey had about an hour to write before the paper's 11 p.m. deadline. "I spent 45 minutes to an hour reporting the story, and less than an hour writing it," he says. The article ran on page 2 the next day and was a Daily News scoop. The city's other papers had to scramble to match Claffey's story, which also got big play on local TV and radio. The media storm prompted the NYPD to launch a full investigation.

But the disappearance of Michael Sullivan and Sylvia Camden remains a mystery to this day. No trace of them was ever found. The couple's landlord was questioned but never arrested in the connection with the case, though he was later convicted on tax evasion charges.

Claffey graduated with a bachelor's degree in English from the University of Chicago in 1984, then worked for several years at a weekly paper that covers civil service issues in New York. He received his master's degree in journalism from Columbia University in 1988, then landed a reporting job at the Daily Press in Newport News, Va., where he covered county government, the police and city hall. Hired on at the Daily News in 1993, Claffey has covered everything from Long Island politics to crime and the courts.

Claffey's advice for writing on deadline? "Don't wait until you've written the perfect lead to write the rest of the story. Do a rough lead, even if it's wordy. You can always polish it later. Highlight the best quotes you have in your notebook right away, then type those into the story."

"Working the graveyard shift is great training at any newspaper," he adds, "because time is tight. Working days it's easy to fritter away your time, but working nights focuses your mind. You get an assignment and the editors are screaming for the story right away. You're always on a tight deadline. Building up your writing speed comes with experience. It's a matter of training your mind and your fingers to work at a certain speed."

Being a reporter is exciting anywhere, but breaking into a big market like New York isn't easy. "You have to pay your dues and be persistent," Claffey says. "Get some training and experience at the entry level. You have to be willing to start at the bottom. Make the most of any opportunity you can get."

Here is Claffey's story as it appeared in the *New York Daily News*.

A lower Manhattan man and his live-in girlfriend have been missing since last week, and neighbors and relatives fear that something may have happened to them while they were out jogging Friday night.

"Their wallets and passports are in the apartment, and the only thing missing is their running shoes and one set of keys," said Chuck Delaney, a neighbor of Michael Sullivan and Camden Sylvia in a loft building at 76 Pearl St.

Sullivan, about 50, is a dancer and choreographer who works at the New Museum downtown. Sylvia, 36, has worked at a Manhattan real estate office for 14 years. Officers from the 1st Precinct visited the apartment and filed a form with the Missing Persons Bureau at the request of Sylvia's mother, Laurie. Laurie Sylvia and neighbors are convinced that the couple would not have skipped town without letting someone know.

"I've known one of these people for 20 years and the other for five years, and I know they didn't blow out to Atlantic City," Delaney said.

"They are missing, and this thing doesn't bode well."

Delaney was contacted Tuesday by friends of Sylvia's from the real estate office. They also reached out for her mother, an activist for the disabled from Hyannis, Mass.

Laurie Sylvia arrived in New York yesterday, and when she looked through the couple's apartment, she found a movie rented Friday afternoon, "Addicted to Love," and fresh food in the fridge.

"She wouldn't rent a movie and then just leave," she said. "She's a very predictable, conscientious person. For her to just leave without telling anyone is totally out of character."

Sullivan is about 5 feet 8, with a wiry build, short gray hair and blue eyes. Sylvia is 5 feet 4, with short, dark hair, blue eyes and dark-framed glasses. She possibly was wearing a black jacket with a bright stripe in the front.

Anyone with information is urged to call the 1st Precinct at (212) 334-0611, or a private number set up by the family, (800) 729-0186, ext. 1155.

New York Daily News, L.P., reprinted with permission.

INTERNET EXERCISES

Many police department Web sites post press releases or arrest/incident reports that can be used as the basis for newswriting exercises. You can call up a report that looks interesting and write a story based on the information provided. Here are a few such sites:

Chicago Police Department **http://www.ci.chi.il.us/CommunityPolicing/AboutCPD/PressReleases/PressReleases.html**

Santa Monica Police Department **http://santamonicapd.org/Press_Info/press_release.htm**

Duluth Police Department **http://www.police.ci.duluth.mn.us/PoliceSite/PressRel.asp**

Davis, Ca., Police Department **http://www.city.davis.ca.us/police/press/**

Franklin, Tenn., Police Department **http://www.franklin-gov.com/Police/PressReleases/PressReleases.htm**

University of Missouri-Columbia Police Department   **http://www.mupolice.com/ pr/index.shtml**

Crime Scene   **http://www.crimescene.com**

The Smoking Gun   **http://www.thesmokinggun.com**, also Court TV **http://www.courttv.com**. Both carry arrest reports from high-profile cases, many involving celebrities.

Web sites operated by the Bureau of Justice Statistics   **http://www.ojp.usdoj. gov/bjs/** and the FBI   **http://www.fbi.gov**. Both have a wealth of statistical data on crime in the United States. Users can access press releases or raw numbers broken down into a variety of categories that can be the basis for news stories.

BEYOND THE CLASSROOM

Visit a local police department headquarters or precinct house. Ask to see the arrest log. From the log, pick an incident that looks interesting, then ask to see the corresponding arrest report. Gather as much information as you can from the arrest report. Then ask to interview one of the officers, preferably one who dealt with the incident you're writing about. If appropriate, interview members of the community where the incident occurred. Write a story.

4

The Courts

Covering the courts is a great beat for any journalist. There are countless moments of intense drama in the courtroom, especially in high-profile cases. One only need look to the O.J. Simpson case and the rise of Court TV to see how big trials can mesmerize the country.

Court reporters must take incredibly complex material—the legal jargon spouted by attorneys, the often-Byzantine workings of the criminal justice system—and make it understandable to the average reader. While covering a big trial can seem glamorous, it's also very hard work. Court reporters typically weed through dozens of run-of-the-mill cases before finding one that interests readers. And a diligent court reporter can fill several notebooks with just one day's worth of trial testimony.

Court reporters, like police reporters, must choose their words carefully. Too often, journalism students covering the courts for the first time make the mistake of writing that a person has committed a crime, when in fact that person is simply on trial but hasn't been convicted of anything. Or they write sentences like, "When convicted, John Doe faces a sentence of five years in prison." Not all defendants who stand trial are convicted, and because of widespread plea-bargaining, many defendants who are charged with one crime will be convicted of less serious offenses.

Court reporters must be absolutely clear about these distinctions and must be especially careful to attribute unproven accusations—also called allegations—to their source. *Prosecutors allege that John Doe killed his wife.* In other words, remember the time-honored phrase, "innocent until proven guilty."

OTHER TIPS

Courtroom dramas are commonplace in movies. Darrell Smith, a reporter who has covered the courts for the Palm Springs Gazette in California, says it helps to think visually. "I think about stories almost like a screenplay," Smith says. "I think of characters and scenes. I think visually when I'm writing because I really do want to paint a picture of what happened." He says reporters should "use the courtroom as a place to tell stories. Look for details, look for little things. So many times court stories read like a baseball game. The judge did this, the defense attorney did that; it becomes formulaic. Try a different approach."

Smith says giving readers the context of the case is also important. "Tell us why the case matters. "And if someone said something particularly interesting, pull that out and use it." For example, Smith once covered a murder trial in which a defense attorney gave a three-and-a-half-hour summation. The attorney argued that the testimony of the prosecution's key witness should be thrown out, saying it was full of holes. To make his point, the attorney told the story of how his daughter had bought a candy bar that was full of wormholes. That was the quote Smith used in his piece.

On a more practical note, Smith says a reporter on the courthouse beat should cultivate a good relationship with the court clerk. "Court clerks are the gatekeepers to all the information in the courthouse. They have access to everything. If you can't get past the clerk you can't get anything. So make the court clerk your best friend," Smith adds. "When Christmas comes, make sure you leave flowers on their desk. Remember their birthdays, make small talk with them. I was able to build relationships with them, and that served me well when I needed to get information."

SOME BASICS OF THE COURT SYSTEM

Every court reporter should understand the workings of the system she is covering. There isn't enough room in this book to cover everything, but here are a few of the basics:

Types of Law

There are two types of law, criminal and civil. Criminal law refers to state or federal prosecutors bringing a case against a person charged with a major crime, also called a felony. As mentioned in Chapter 2, felonies fall into two categories—violent crime and property crime. Violent crime includes murder, rape, robbery and aggravated assault. Property crime includes burglary, larceny-theft, and motor vehicle theft. Civil law deals with lawsuits brought by individuals against other individuals, organizations or companies. Criminal cases by their very nature tend to be more newsworthy than civil cases, though there are certainly exceptions to this rule.

Structure of the Court System

The court system is composed of two branches, state and federal. The two branches operate separately and are independent of the executive and legislative branches of government.

STATE   The lowest state courts may include county, municipal, traffic, magistrate, justice of the peace and police courts. These courts handle minor cases and arraignments.

More serious offenses are heard in superior court, also known as state district court or circuit court. State superior courts hear appeals from the lower courts and are where most of the nation's trials are held.

The highest state court is often called the state supreme court. It generally hears appeals from the state superior courts. States usually also operate special courts, including juvenile, divorce, family, housing and small-claims courts.

FEDERAL   The federal court system begins with the federal district courts. These hear cases relating to alleged violations of the Constitution or other federal laws. There is at least one federal district court in each of the 50 states.

The United States courts of appeals hear appeals from the federal district courts. These courts also hear cases involving a challenge to an order of a federal regulatory agency, such as the Securities and Exchange Commission.

The highest court in the federal system, and indeed the country, is the United States Supreme Court. The Supreme Court can review rulings made by the U.S. courts of appeals, or hear appeals from state appellate courts if a constitutional issue is involved. The Supreme Court has final jurisdiction on all cases it hears.

Like the state courts, the federal system includes specialized courts such as the U.S. Court of International Trade and the Tax Court.

Terms

Court reporters must master legalese, the jargon spoken by attorneys, judges and officers of the court. Here are a few key terms:

Acquit   To render a verdict of not guilty.

Allege   To assert something without proof. *Prosecutors allege that he killed his wife.*

Appeals court   A court that reviews lower court rulings.

Arraignment   A court hearing at which a defendant is formally charged with a crime or crimes and bail is set.

Arrest   The seizure of a person based on the suspicion that he or she has committed a crime.

Bail   Money paid by the defendant to ensure his or her appearance at trial.

Defendant   A person who is charged with a crime in a criminal case or is the party being sued in a civil case.

District attorney   An officer who brings cases against defendants on behalf of the government.

Felony   Serious crimes like murder or robbery, as opposed to misdemeanors. Felonies are generally punishable by more than a year in prison.

Grand jury   A jury whose job is to decide whether there is enough evidence to go to trial. (Grand jury proceedings are closed to the public and the press.)

Hung jury   A jury that cannot reach a verdict; this generally results in the case being retried or dropped.

Indictment   The document handed up to the court by a grand jury that charges a defendant with a crime.

Misdemeanor   A criminal offense that is less serious than a felony.

No bill   A grand jury finding that there is insufficient evidence to support charges being filed.

Plaintiff   The person who files a lawsuit.

Plea bargain   A deal between prosecutors and the defense in which the defendant pleads guilty to a lesser crime in exchange for a reduced sentence.

Preliminary hearing   A hearing at which the judge listens to evidence to determine whether the case should proceed to trial. This comes after the arraignment.

Subpoena   A document issued by a judge to force a witness to testify in court.

True bill   A grand jury finding that there is sufficient evidence to put the defendant on trial.

exercise one

Write a story based on the following information. Deadline: 30 minutes.

Case background: Jason Belker, 25, arrested yesterday for allegedly shooting a clerk at a SuperMart convenience store during a robbery last Tuesday. The clerk, Peter Tyson, was shot in the shoulder but managed to give police a description of the suspect. Surveillance cameras also caught him on tape. Belker was arrested when he was stopped for a broken taillight and a highway patrol officer recognized him. A gun found in Belker's car, a .22-caliber pistol, was later identified through ballistics testing as the one used in the robbery. Belker is being arraigned today before Centerville District Court Judge Patricia Jacobsen on charges of attempted murder and armed robbery. Belker's court-appointed attorney, Jerry Fincher, enters a plea of not guilty on his client's behalf. Jacobsen orders Belker held on $1 million bail. He'll remain in custody at the Centerville Correctional Center. Assistant District Attorney Janet Simpson tells you Belker is a drifter who has a rap sheet that includes previous convictions for burglary and drug possession.

exercise two

Write a story based on the following information. Deadline: 30 minutes.

Two months have passed since Belker's arrest, and his trial is today. Testimony lasts through the morning and most of the afternoon; the prosecution's main witness is Tyson, the clerk, who from the witness stand positively identifies Belker as the man who shot him. Tyson says his wound has healed but he is still recovering. "I have nightmares all the time about what happened," he says tearfully in court. "My life still isn't back to normal." Fincher, Belker's attorney, tries to poke holes in Tyson's account by pointing out that he wears thick glasses and is nearsighted. But after getting the case late this afternoon, the jury deliberates just over two hours before finding Belker guilty of attempted murder and armed robbery. Superior Court Judge John Pembroke schedules sentencing for tomorrow morning.

exercise three

Write a story based on the following information. Deadline: 30 minutes.

It's sentencing day for Belker. In a statement he reads in court, he says, "I'm sorry for what I've done. I didn't mean to hurt anyone. I want to apologize to Mr. Tyson and his family." Superior Court Judge John Pembroke tells Belker, "Sir, you're a young man and already you have a string of criminal convictions. With this latest crime you've shown that you are a danger to society." Pembroke sentences Belker to 10 to 25 years in the state prison at Delward. Assistant District Attorney Janet Simpson tells you Belker will be eligible for parole in about seven years.

exercise four

Write a story based on the information found in this indictment from the U.S. Attorney's Office in Philadelphia. Deadline: 45 minutes. Note: The names of the defendants in this document have been changed.

IN THE UNITED STATES DISTRICT COURT

FOR THE EASTERN DISTRICT OF PENNSYLVANIA

UNITED STATES OF AMERICA :

v. :

MIKE SMITH :

LAMAR BEMLER :

DATE FILED:

CRIM. NO.:

VIOLATIONS: 18 U.S.C. §371 (conspiracy—1 Count)

18 U.S.C. §2114 (robbery of property of the United States—1 Count)

18 U.S.C. § 2 (aiding and abetting)

INDICTMENT

COUNT ONE

THE GRAND JURY CHARGES THAT:

1. On or about November 20, 2001, at Ambler, in the Eastern District of Pennsylvania, defendants MIKE SMITH and LAMAR BEMLER conspired and agreed with each other and others, including James Robertson (charged elsewhere) to rob the Ambler, Pennsylvania post office in violation of Title 18, Section 2114(a).

MANNER AND MEANS OF THE CONSPIRACY

It was the manner and means of the conspiracy that:

2. Defendants MIKE SMITH and LAMAR BEMLER, together with

James Robertson, would obtain money by robbing a post office.

OVERT ACTS

The defendants performed or caused someone else to perform the following overt acts in the Eastern District of Pennsylvania on November 20, 2001 in furtherance of the conspiracy:

1. Defendant MIKE SMITH drove defendant LAMAR BEMLER and James Robertson to the Ambler Post Office in Ambler, Pennsylvania.

2. Defendant LAMAR BEMLER waited in the car as the get-away driver.

3. Defendant MIKE SMITH and James Robertson waited by the rear door of the post office for workers to leave at the end of the business day.

4. Defendant MIKE SMITH donned a mask just before entering the post office.

5. James Robertson followed defendant MIKE SMITH into the post office to prevent anyone from stopping defendant SMITH.

6. Defendant MIKE SMITH grabbed two post office satchels containing cash and checks as

he ran through the post office and out the front door.

7. James Robertson got into a fight with two postal workers who tried to stop defendant MIKE SMITH.

8. Defendants MIKE SMITH and LAMAR BEMLER escaped in the car.

9. James Robertson escaped by bus after freeing himself from the two postal workers.

10. Defendants MIKE SMITH and LAMAR BEMLER, together with James Robertson, divided the proceeds.

In violation of Title 18, United States Code, Section 371.

COUNT TWO

THE GRAND JURY FURTHER CHARGES THAT:

On or about November 20, 2001, at the Ambler Post Office, in the Eastern District of

Pennsylvania, defendants MIKE SMITH and LAMAR BEMLER robbed, and aided and abetted the robbery of, United States Postal Service employees having lawful charge, control, and custody of money of the United States.

In violation of Title 18, United States Code, Sections 2114, 2.

A TRUE BILL:

_____

GRAND JURY FOREPERSON

_____

PATRICK L. MEEHAN

United States Attorney

exercise five

Write a story based on the information found in this indictment from the U.S. Attorney's Office in Philadelphia. Deadline: 45 minutes. Note: The names of the defendants in this document have been changed.

IN THE UNITED STATES DISTRICT COURT

FOR THE EASTERN DISTRICT OF PENNSYLVANIA

UNITED STATES OF AMERICA : CRIMINAL NO. _____

v. : DATE FILED: _____

JOHN SMITH : VIOLATIONS: 18 U.S.C. § 1951

GEORGE MILLER (Conspiracy to commit: robbery—1 Count)

(Interference with commerce by robbery—1 Count)

: 18 U.S.C. § 924(c)

(Use of gun during crime of violence—1 Count)

: 18 U.S.C. § 922(g)(1)

(Possession of firearm by convicted felon—2 Counts)

18 U.S.C. § 2

: (Aiding and abetting)

INDICTMENT

COUNT ONE

THE GRAND JURY CHARGES THAT:

1. At all times material to the Indictment, West Coast Video, located at 1216 Liberty Street, Allentown, Pennsylvania, was a business engaged in interstate commerce.

2. On or about June 12, 2002, in Allentown, in the Eastern District of Pennsylvania, defendants

JOHN SMITH

GEORGE MILLER

conspired and agreed together to unlawfully obstruct, delay and affect commerce, and the movement of articles and commodities in commerce, by robbery, as that term is defined in Title 18, United States Code, Section 1951(b)(1), in that the defendants agreed to unlawfully take United States currency belonging to West Coast Video located at 1216 Liberty Street, Allentown, Pennsylvania, from the care, custody, control, management, and possession of West Coast Video's employees, in the presence of the employees, against their will, by means of actual and threatened force, violence, and fear of injury, immediate and future, to their person, all in violation of Title 18, United States Code, Section 1951.

THE MANNER AND MEANS OF THE CONSPIRACY

3. It was part of the conspiracy that defendants JOHN SMITH and GEORGE MILLER planned and executed the armed robbery of West Coast Video, by use of force, threats of force and violence, and through the use of a firearm.

OVERT ACTS

1. On or about June 12, 2002, defendants JOHN SMITH and GEORGE MILLER entered the West Coast Video to commit an armed robbery. MILLER, displaying a handgun, threatened to shoot the store's patrons and employees to intimidate the victims present in the store.

2. On or about June 12, 2002, defendant GEORGE MILLER held the store employees and patrons at gunpoint while SMITH and MILLER stole approximately $551 from the cash register.

3. On or about June 12, 2002, defendant JOHN SMITH told defendant GEORGE MILLER to shoot one of the store's patrons to intimidate the victims present in the store.

4. On or about June 12, 2002, defendants JOHN SMITH and GEORGE MILLER ran from the West Coast Video into a cemetery in Allentown to avoid apprehension.

All in violation of Title 18, United States Code, Section 1951.

COUNT TWO

THE GRAND JURY FURTHER CHARGES THAT:

On or about June 12, 2002, in Allentown, Lehigh County, in the Eastern District of Pennsylvania, defendants

JOHN SMITH

GEORGE MILLER

did unlawfully obstruct, delay and affect commerce, as that term is defined in Title 18, United States Code, Section 1951(b)(3), and the movement of articles and commodities in commerce, by robbery, as that term is defined in Title 18, United States Code, Section 1951(b)(1), in that the defendants did unlawfully take and obtain, and aid and abet the taking and obtaining of, property, that is approximately $551 in United States currency, belonging to West Coast Video located at 1216 Liberty Street, Allentown, Pennsylvania, from the care, custody, control, management, and possession of West Coast Video's employees, in the presence of the employees, against their will, by means of actual and threatened force, violence, and fear of injury, immediate and future, to their person.

In violation of Title 18, United States Code, Section 1951 and Section 2.

COUNT THREE

THE GRAND JURY FURTHER CHARGES THAT:

On or about June 12, 2002, in Allentown, Lehigh County, in the Eastern District of Pennsylvania, defendants

JOHN SMITH

GEORGE MILLER

did knowingly use and carry, and aid and abet the use and carrying of, a firearm during and in relation to a crime of violence, that is Hobbs Act robbery as charged in Count Two of this Indictment.

In violation of Title 18, United States Code, Section 924(c)(1) and Section 2.

COUNT FOUR

THE GRAND JURY FURTHER CHARGES THAT:

On or about June 12, 2002, in Allentown, Lehigh County, in the Eastern District of Pennsylvania, defendant

GEORGE MILLER

having been previously convicted of an offense punishable by imprisonment for a term exceeding one year, knowingly possessed in and affecting interstate commerce a firearm.

In violation of Title 18, United States Code, Section 922(g)(1).

COUNT FIVE

THE GRAND JURY FURTHER CHARGES THAT:

On or about June 12, 2002, in Allentown, Lehigh County, in the Eastern District of Pennsylvania, defendant

JOHN SMITH

having been previously convicted of an offense punishable by imprisonment for a term exceeding one year, knowingly possessed, and aided and abetted the possession, in and affecting interstate commerce a firearm.

In violation of Title 18, United States Code, Section 922(g)(1) and Section 2.

A TRUE BILL:

_____

FOREPERSON

_____

PATRICK L. MEEHAN
United States Attorney

exercise six

Write a story based on the information found in this indictment from the U.S. Attorney's Office in Philadelphia. Deadline: one hour. Note: The name of the defendant in this document has been changed.

IN THE UNITED STATES DISTRICT COURT

FOR THE EASTERN DISTRICT OF PENNSYLVANIA

UNITED STATES OF AMERICA : CRIMINAL NO._____

v.

MELVIN JURGENSEN : DATE FILED:_____

: VIOLATIONS: 18 U.S.C. § 371

(Conspiracy to commit armed bank robbery—1 count) 18 U.S.C. § 2113(d)

(Armed bank robbery—1 count)

18 U.S.C. § 924(c)

(Using a firearm during a crime of violence – 1 count)

18 U.S.C. § 2

(Aiding and abetting)

I N D I C T M E N T

COUNT ONE

THE GRAND JURY CHARGES THAT:

On or about September 4, 2002, at Bethlehem Township, Pennsylvania, in the Eastern District of Pennsylvania, the defendant **MELVIN JURGENSEN** conspired and agreed together with another person, to commit an offense against the United States, that is, to knowingly and unlawfully commit

armed bank robbery, in violation of Title 18, United States Code, Section 2113(d).

MANNER AND MEANS

1. It was part of the conspiracy that the defendant MELVIN JURGENSEN agreed with another person to commit an armed bank robbery at the Heights St. Joseph Federal Credit Union, located at 3530 Freemansburg Avenue, Bethlehem Township, Pennsylvania, a financial institution the deposits of which were insured by the Federal Deposit Insurance Corporation (FDIC).

OVERT ACTS

In furtherance of the conspiracy, the defendant committed the following overt acts in the Eastern District of Pennsylvania:

1. On or about September 4, 2002, at approximately 2 p.m., defendant MELVIN JURGENSEN and another person went together and entered the Heights St. Joseph Federal Credit Union, located at 3530 Freemansburg Avenue, Bethlehem Township, Pennsylvania, for the purpose of committing an armed bank robbery.

2. On or about September 4, 2002, the defendant MELVIN JURGENSEN and another person entered the bank wearing nylon stocking masks, and vaulted the teller counter. One of the robbers brandished a dark, long barreled revolver and ordered the bank employees, at gunpoint, to get down on the ground.

3. One of the robbers ordered a bank employee, at gunpoint, by physically placing the gun into the bank employee's back, to go

to the bank vault and open the safe where the money was being stored.

4. While committing the armed bank robbery, one of the robbers took a plastic trash bag with yellow ties from a garbage can inside the bank, and used it to put the bank money into, which was bundled in bank wrappers, so the money could be carried out of the bank.

5. The defendant MELVIN JURGENSEN and another person stole approximately $37,555 of U.S. currency from the bank, much of which was still bundled in the bank wrappers of the Heights St. Joseph Federal Credit Union.

6. On or about September 6, 2002, defendant MELVIN JURGENSEN was in possession of approximately $7,578 of the stolen bank money, much of which was still in bundles secured by bank wrappers of the Heights St. Joseph Federal Credit Union.

7. It was a further part of the conspiracy that the defendant MELVIN JURGENSEN used a rented green Kia, PA Reg. EDH-6043, as the getaway car to flee from the scene after committing the armed bank robbery.

All in violation of Title 18, United States Code, Section 371.

COUNT TWO

THE GRAND JURY FURTHER CHARGES THAT:

On or about September 4, 2002, at Bethlehem Township, Pennsylvania, in the Eastern District of Pennsylvania, the defendant

MELVIN JURGENSEN

knowingly and unlawfully, by force and violence, and by intimidation, did take, and did aid and abet the taking, from employees of the Heights St. Joseph Federal Credit Union, located at 3530 Freemansburg Avenue, Bethlehem Township, Pennsylvania, lawful currency of the United States, that is, approximately $37,555.00 cash, belonging to, and in the care, custody, control,

management and possession of the Heights St. Joseph Federal Credit Union, a financial institution the deposits of which were and are insured by the Federal Deposit Insurance Corporation (FDIC) and, in so doing, defendant **MELVIN JURGENSEN** and another person did knowingly and unlawfully assault and put in jeopardy the lives of the employees of the Heights St. Joseph Federal Credit Union, and others, by use of a dangerous weapon, that is, a firearm described as a dark long barreled revolver.

In violation of Title 18, United States Code, Sections 2113(d) and 2.

COUNT THREE

THE GRAND JURY FURTHER CHARGES THAT:

On or about September 4, 2002, at Bethlehem Township, Pennsylvania, in the Eastern District of Pennsylvania, the defendant

MELVIN JURGENSEN

knowingly used and carried a firearm, and aided and abetted the using and carrying of a firearm, that is, a dark long barreled revolver, during and in relation to a crime of violence for which they may be prosecuted in a Court of the United States, that is, armed bank robbery of the Heights St. Joseph Federal Credit Union, located at 3530 Freemansburg Avenue, Bethlehem Township, Pennsylvania, in violation of Title 18, United States Code, Section 2113(d), as charged in Count Two of this Indictment.

In violation of Title 18, United States Code, Sections 924(c)(1)(A)(i) and (ii) and 2.

A TRUE BILL:

_____

FOREPERSON

_____

PATRICK L. MEEHAN
United States Attorney

Real REPORTER: Darrell Smith

It was the biggest story of 26-year-old Darrell Smith's young journalism career, and one that would shake his hometown to its core.

On a spring afternoon in the sleepy California town of Yuba City, 8-year-old Michael Lyons disappeared somewhere in the few short blocks between his school and his home in an apartment complex. At first Michael's parents thought he was with friends. But by 5:30 that afternoon they began to worry. Police and an army of volunteers launched a search of the area that evening. Their efforts reached a horrifying end the next morning, when Michael's body was found a few miles from his home, in a marshy spot on the banks of the Feather River. He had been stabbed more than 70 times and sexually assaulted.

A few hours later, police arrested Robert Boyd Rhoades in the same area. Prosecutors eventually linked the 43-year-old convicted child molester to Michael's brutal slaying, and when Rhoades was hauled into court, the whole town was watching.

Smith, a reporter for the Marysville Appeal-Democrat, the area's main daily paper, was assigned to cover Rhoades' arraignment. Smith was a native of the area, so he felt extra pressure to get the story right. "I knew I needed to be on my toes," Smith says. "This was a story that affected an entire community. I didn't want to let anybody down."

But crafting an exceptional story from an arraignment is never easy. An arraignment is simply a hearing in which a defendant is formally charged with a crime. Sometimes the defendant enters a plea, but often that occurs at a later hearing. Not much else happens at arraignments, so they tend to be short—usually just a matter of minutes. Smith needed to do more than simply describe the legal proceedings.

"I knew I couldn't cover this as a routine arraignment," Smith says. "I wanted to focus on the little details that could tell the story. "The family was there, the police were there, it was very emotional," he adds. "I wanted to try to capture that emotion and set the scene."

Smith scribbled notes furiously, jotting down descriptions of the packed courtroom, the grieving family members and the sheriff's deputies circling the room to provide extra security. When Rhoades was led into court, Smith noted that his hands and feet were shackled, and that he was brought in from a side entrance. And when Sandy Friend, the mother of the murdered boy, broke down and wept, Smith put that in his notes as well.

"I tried to look for as many details as possible, to really listen to what was going on," Smith says. "Usually in a more routine court case you get caught up in legal proceedings— what the judge said, what the defense attorney said. Here I was looking more, trying to be more observational. I especially wanted to focus on the boy's mother and on the police chaplain who was with her, on the way Rhoades walked into the courtroom, things like that."

The arraignment was over quickly. As soon as it ended, Smith grabbed several people for brief interviews, then rushed back to the newsroom. It was still early, but Smith, a reporter on a small paper with a staff of only seven reporters, knew he might have to write two or three more stories that day. There was no time to waste. "I really had to get back [to the newsroom] quickly. As I was taking down notes I was already thinking of how the story would be organized. I knew certain quotes and details would stand out. So by the time I got into my car and got back to the office, I'd had time to think about how to structure the story."

For Smith, building a mental framework for a story—even before he's written a single word—is a must when working on a tight deadline. "I want to have an idea of what the story will be even before I cover it. I'm not presupposing what the story will be, but I'm setting a structure, a framework. I continue to observe and listen, to get the details. But with a framework I'm not going to have to come back to the office and go through page after page of notes to figure out what I want to write."

Smith also says that once he begins writing, he self-edits his copy as he goes along. "As you're writing you're thinking, 'Is this strong enough? Is it too strong? Is it dramatic without being maudlin? Is this saying what happened or what I want it to say?' You ask yourself those questions throughout the process and hopefully come to a place where you're satisfied that that's what happened."

Smith says working at a small paper where had to write several stories a day was great training. "Having to write two or three stories a day, you learn pretty quickly how to prioritize. I used to spend two or three hours on each story. It would take me much longer than it should have. Writing on deadline is like exercise," he adds. "You've got to work those muscles to a point where you know you can turn out the copy much more quickly."

Smith, a California native, says he's wanted to be a reporter since the fourth grade. He wrote for his high school and college newspapers, then left college in his junior year to take on his first professional writing job—covering off-road racing for "Dusty Times" magazine. Since then he's worked on an Air Force base newspaper, edited a business publication and been a reporter at several papers in California and Colorado. He's currently a columnist and reporter for the Desert Sun newspaper in Palm Springs, Ca.

Rhoades, meanwhile, was convicted of killing Michael Lyons. He is on death row. Here is the story Darrell Smith wrote on the Rhoades arraignment.

The case of the People v. Robert Boyd Rhoades took its first steps Thursday morning with the accused killer's arraignment amid tight security at the Sutter County Courthouse.

"This is the first step in a long journey we'll all take together. Quite frankly, it's a small step," said Sutter County Consolidated Court Judge Robert Damron, charged to hear the first capital case in Sutter County in nearly 20 years.

That journey will continue Aug. 15 when Rhoades enters his plea in a Sutter County Courtroom. On the advice of his attorney, Robert Spangler, Rhoades reserved his plea until the August court date.

Rhoades, formally charged Wednesday with the kidnapping and murder of 8-year-old Michael Lyons of Yuba City two months ago, faces the death penalty in connection with the brutal slaying.

As Sutter County sheriff's deputies ringed the perimeter or the courtroom, Rhoades, his hands and feet shackled, was led silently through a side entrance to his seat in the front of the courtroom for the unusual 11 a.m. arraignment.

Meanwhile, in the back row of the courtroom, Lyons' mother, Sandy Friend, and other members of Lyons' family grimly looked on as Rhoades was led into the room to await his arraignment.

As Damron methodically read the five-page complaint, the final hours of Michael Lyons' life came into horribly sharp focus.

Torture. Sodomy. Lewd acts. Murder.

Sandra Friend tried vainly to hold back her tears as the charges were read before finally succumbing to her emotion. Behind Friend, hands on her shoulders, was Yuba City Police Chaplain Lewis McElfresh.

Meanwhile, Rhoades, sitting next to Spangler, looked nervously about the courtroom before the complaint was read.

In all, the 43-year-old convicted child molester faces seven counts including first-degree murder, kidnapping, torture, sodomy, lewd acts and oral copulation in connection with Lyons' death.

Those charges also carry special circumstances of kidnapping, sodomy, lewd and lascivious acts with a child under 14 years of age and murder by torture.

After the early morning hearing, Spangler said the charges against his client were "inappropriate" and voiced concerns about the publicity the case has garnered, but would not say whether he will seek to move the trial out of Sutter County.

"These are inappropriate charges. We're going to look at it and review the charges," Spangler said. "Mr. Rhoades is shocked that he's being charged with this and feels he will be vindicated. We anticipate a not guilty plea."

Lyons was found dead in dense overgrowth and brush along the banks of the Feather River nearly a day after he was declared missing May 16 when he failed to return home from Yuba City's Bridge Street School.

The search brought together an army of Yuba City police, FBI agents, municipal workers and volunteers in hopes of finding the young Lyons alive.

Rhoades was located several hours later near where Lyons' body was found and was arrested by Sutter County sheriff's deputies on a parole violation for carrying a knife with a blade more than 2 inches in length.

Rhoades' parole has since been revoked and he is being held without bail at Yuba County Jail.

Reprinted with permission from the Marysville Appeal-Democrat.

INTERNET EXERCISES

Many court records and documents available online can be used as the basis for newswriting exercises. Here are a few Web sites where court records, including indictments of the type seen in this chapter, can be found:

Findlaw   **http://www.findlaw.com**

U.S. Attorney's Office for the Eastern District of Pennsylvania   **http://www.usao-edpa.com/**

U.S. Attorney's Office for the Eastern District of Louisiana   **http://www.usaoedla.com/frameset.htm**

Kane County State's Attorney's Office (Illinois)   **http://www.co.kane.il.us/sao/**

U.S. Attorney's Office, District of New Jersey   **http://www.njusao.org**

The Smoking Gun (court documents relating to celebrity arrests)   **http://www.thesmokinggun.com**

BEYOND THE CLASSROOM

1. Visit your local courthouse and cover a preliminary hearing, an arraignment, and several hours of testimony in a criminal trial.
2. Visit the court clerk's office and ask to see the documents for a civil suit. Contact the attorneys involved on both sides of the case and write a story based on the documents you find and the interviews you conduct.

5

Fire
and Rescue

*r*eporters covering the local fire department and emergency rescue services deal with many of the same issues faced by police reporters. In fact, on many smaller newspapers, police reporters are also responsible for fire and rescue coverage. The beats are similar: lots of breaking news stories, many involving life-or-death situations that must be covered on very short notice. After all, fires and plane crashes don't occur on any sort of schedule.

Reporters covering emergency situations like these must always keep in mind that human life—and death—are of paramount importance in any news story. If a person is injured or killed, that must be in the lead. In fact, there's an old newsroom saying that goes, "no stiff, no story." Obviously that's not always the case, but it points up the importance of making sure that any loss of life is at the top of the story. Property damage is also important, particularly if it involves the destruction of large structures worth lots of money. But the human element always comes first.

Reporters must be particularly careful with the facts. In the immediate aftermath of something like a fire or a plane crash, the situation is usually chaotic. Information—some reliable, some not—flies at the reporter from many directions. Find the person in charge of the situation—a fire marshal, for instance—and look to him for solid information on the five W's and the H of the story. Eyewitnesses can provide dramatic quotes and color for a story, but be wary of speculation, especially about the *causes* of things. An eyewitness may swear to a reporter that he saw a plane's engine explode in flames before it crashed, but until a thorough investigation has been completed, no one—not even that eyewitness—can say for certain what caused the plane to plummet to the ground.

exercise one

Write a story based on this press release from the Centerville Fire Department. Deadline: 20 minutes.

At 3:34 a.m. the department responded to a reported grass fire near the railroad tracks behind Jackson's Bar and Grill on 3071 Torrance Road. Firefighters found a male adult on fire. An ambulance was called. The man was identified as William Grimes, age 42. He was transported to St. Mary's Hospital with second-degree burns to his hands, arms and face and is in stable condition. Preliminary investigation shows the fire was started accidentally. Early indications were that Grimes was too close to his bonfire when his clothing ignited. No other damage or injuries were reported. Grimes was apparently homeless and had been living in a cardboard box near the railroad tracks for the past several weeks.

exercise two

Write a story based on this fire department press release. Deadline: 20 minutes.

At 4:43 p.m. today the Centerville Fire Department responded to a report of raw sewage spilling from a sewage line underneath O'-Malley's pub at 2709 Towson Road. Firefighters found the sewage was spilling down an embankment and into the Blue River. A preliminary investigation found that the pub's sewer system consists of a pump that normally pumps sewage into the main sewer lines near Towson Road. But the pump apparently malfunctioned, causing the spill. A Hazmat Team was able to fix the pump, stopping the spill. Firefighters estimated that about 2,000 pounds of raw sewage had spilled into the Blue River.

Write a story based on this Centerville Fire Department press release. Deadline: 30 minutes.

Firefighters dispatched to a motor vehicle accident with entrapment at the intersection of State St. and Carville Ave. at 1:32 a.m. this morning. The car traveling east on State struck the rear of an oil truck stopped at the intersection's stop light. The force of the impact drove the bumper of the car up to the rear wheels of the tanker. The car's dashboard was pushed back and down, trapping the driver beneath the dash on the floor. Eyewitnesses reported that the victim was barely visible but was fully alert and talking. Firefighters used extrication tools including hydraulic spreaders, rams and cutters to remove the roof and raise the dash enough to extricate the victim. It took approximately 30 minutes to extricate the heavily entrapped woman. The driver of the truck was taken to St. Luke's Hospital with only minor injuries from the accident. He's identified as Timothy Smockton, 32, of Centerville.

Write a story based on these notes from an interview with Fire Capt. George Russell of the Centerville Fire Department. Deadline: 30 minutes.

Fire broke out about 2:30 a.m. in a three-story rowhouse in Blyburg Heights, a working-class section of the city. Address is 1387 Smithson Road. Firefighters were on the scene within about five minutes of getting the call. They brought fire under control in about 30 minutes; managed to prevent blaze from spreading to adjacent row homes. Most damage was in the building's third floor, which will need extensive repairs. Damage estimated at about $80,000. Fire appeared to start on the third floor; preliminary investigation shows it started when an adult in that apartment fell asleep while smoking. Building had three separate apartments, with 12 residents total; they are being sheltered by Red Cross and relatives. All escaped unhurt except a 3-year-old child on the third floor, who's listed in critical condition at St. Mary's Hospital with severe smoke inhalation.

Later, Russell calls back. He says the person who started the fire with a cigarette is Jerry Timsfield. The child who is hospitalized is his son, James. Russell says Timsfield tried to rescue his son but couldn't find him in the smoke. Firefighters managed to rescue the child, but not before he suffered smoke inhalation.

Write a story based on these notes from your interviews with Capt. Bill Jackson of the Centerville Fire Department and Lt. Mike O'Malley of the Centerville Police Department. Deadline: 30 minutes.

According to Capt. Jackson, a fire broke out at about 11:45 p.m. last night in a wooden rowhouse in Blyburg Heights. There are four separate apartments in the building. All the residents managed to escape, and no one was injured. Firefighters doused the blaze within 30 minutes. But the fire gutted the building, causing an estimated $200,000 in damage, and all 18 occupants were left homeless. Some stayed with relatives; others were helped by the Red Cross.

Lt. O'Malley says the entrance of the building is a known hangout for crack dealers and users. He says several people were seen running from the building after the fire began, and police are looking for them. O'Malley concludes, "I think this fire was started by drug users who dropped a lit crack pipe."

In a phone call to Jackson, he says his preliminary investigation does show that the fire apparently started in the building's entrance area. He says he can't be sure the fire was caused by a lit crack pipe until he does more investigating, but adds, "It wouldn't surprise me if that's how this fire began. We've seen several fires recently caused by drug users."

You hear a lot of chatter on the police scanner about a plane crash and start making phone calls. You must bang out a quick story before heading to the scene. Write a story based on the following notes. Deadline: 30 minutes.

Centerville Fire Department Lt. Betty Franken says the plane crashed about 10 minutes ago, at 10:36 p.m.; was apparently trying to land at Centerville Airport but crashed in a field about a mile from the airport. Fire and rescue crews are just arriving at the scene.

Called the home number of Andy Johnson, a contact at the regional office of the Federal Aviation Administration. He says the plane was an MD-83 passenger jet operated by Galaxy Airlines, flight number 562, en route from Chicago to Centerville; 88 people were onboard, including crew.

In a follow-up call to Lt. Franken, she says the jet's wreckage is spread out over several hundred yards. There's still a lot of fire and smoke, making it difficult for rescue crews to look for survivors. "But so far, we haven't seen any survivors," she says. "It's a grim scene."

The city editor hears some chatter on the police scanner and yells at you to get out to Blue River, near the 1100 block of Padgett Road. Write a story based on your notes taken at the scene. Deadline: one hour.

Several ambulances and squad cars are parked near the riverbank. A child has fallen through the ice about 30 feet out. He's clinging to a chunk of ice but his torso and legs are underwater. The ice appears thin. It's January, and the water is frigid. Also, Blue River has a surprisingly strong current; if the boy falls through, he could easily be swept away. Several EMTs and a cop have spread themselves out flat on the ice and are inching toward the boy, who is screaming and crying. The rescuers are holding onto each other's feet, creating a human chain, so that if the ice breaks again they won't fall through as well. The boy's mother is on the bank, weeping hysterically. Slowly the rescuers crawl toward the boy until the one nearest to him grabs the boy and hauls him out of the water. A group of several dozen onlookers applauds. The boy is quickly wrapped in a blanket and rushed into the ambulance, which speeds away. The weeping mother follows the ambulance to the hospital. An interview with the EMT who hauled the boy from the water, Philip Washington, age 27, reveals, "We got the call and came out as fast as we could. When we saw him out there we knew the only way to reach him in time would be to flatten ourselves out, spread out our weight and move across the ice very slowly, so we wouldn't break it. I just hope the kid's all right." Washington also says he's been an EMT for five years.

Jane Coughlin, 42, who lives in the neighborhood, says: "I always worry about kids on the river. It seems like the ice is never as strong as it looks. But I'm glad the paramedics were here. They're heroes, as far as I'm concerned."

Back at the newsroom a call to Fire Capt. George Russell reveals that the boy's name is Johnny Peterson, age 7. Mother's name is Theresa. Family lives in Centerville. He says Johnny is in good condition at St. Mary's Hospital with hypothermia. "Looks like he'll be fine," Russell says.

Real REPORTER: Harry Yanoshak

Deadline newswriting is often a team effort. When a dump truck smashed into a couple of cars and a bank on an August morning in Newtown, Pa., several young reporters from the Bucks County Courier Times were dispatched to the scene. But they had trouble getting information from police and fire officials about how the crash had occurred. So Harry Yanoshak, one of the paper's more experienced reporters, was sent to the scene to help out.

"There were two reporters already there, but they were striking out in terms of getting some of the information we needed," recalls Yanoshak. "The mechanics of this accident were complicated, and we needed to show our readers exactly what had happened."

Yanoshak found a chaotic scene. Dozens of reporters and spectators surrounded the crash site where rescue crews were extracting crash victims from their vehicles. TV news helicopters buzzed overhead. "We'd seen the damage in a helicopter shot on TV, so we had a general idea of what the scene looked like," Yanoshak says. "But when I got there I couldn't believe how spectacular the damage was."

By interviewing fire and rescue officials at the scene, Yanoshak was able to piece together a chronology of the story. The dump truck, whose driver had lost control of his vehicle, had first smashed into a car, killing an elderly woman. The truck then plowed over a second car, seriously injuring another motorist, then jumped the curb and slammed into the side of a bank.

By the time Yanoshak had completed his reporting and headed back to the newsroom it was early afternoon. He had to quickly type out a short story for the paper's Web site (something newspaper reporters are increasingly required to do), then bang out a more complete account for the paper's early edition, which had a 3 p.m. deadline. Yanoshak's reporting was combined with information gathered by several other reporters to create a comprehensive account of the tragic accident. "I wrote a lot of it, then stuff from other people was wrapped into it," he says. "It was totally a group effort." The teamwork paid off. The Courier Times' coverage of the crash was awarded second place for deadline newswriting in 2001 by the Greater Philadelphia Chapter of the Society of Professional Journalists.

Yanoshak, the Courier Times' crime and public safety reporter, received a bachelor's degree in environmental resources management, then got his master's degree in journalism from Penn State University in 1992. Before joining the Courier Times in 2000, he'd worked at several other papers, including the Intelligencer in Doylestown, Pa.

Yanoshak's beat involves a fair bit of tight-deadline writing. So he's learned a few tricks for turning out clean copy quickly. "You should think about the story as you're going to the scene," he says. "After you've done this awhile you know there are certain categories you can fit a story into. You know it will either be a fire story or a crash story or something like that. You don't assume things, but you're prepared before you get there," he adds. "As you gather your notes you're putting the structure of the story into your head. On the drive back to the office you're thinking, where do I start and where is this going? You develop the outline of the story on that drive. You put the story together in your head and once you get to the computer terminal, you just start writing."

Yanoshak also says he avoids editing himself too much while he's writing. "Just get your thoughts into the computer. Be thorough." But once the story is sent to the editor, "be sure to help out in the editing process. Be there with them so nothing in the story gets screwed up."

Here is the Courier Times' main story on the dump truck crash as it appeared in the paper on Friday, Aug. 4, 2000:

A 77-year-old Newtown Township woman is dead and another is in serious condition after a dump truck went out of control yesterday morning, hitting two cars before running into a bank wall at the Village of Newtown Shopping Center.

Barbara J. Sutcliffe of Society Place was pronounced dead at the scene.

Police and witnesses say the accident occurred at 9:36 a.m. when the truck, heading south on Eagle Road, rear-ended a Lincoln Continental driven by Sutcliffe. She was either stopped at the light or proceeding slowly through the intersection at Durham Road, said police.

The truck pushed the car through the intersection, where it flipped, landing on a sidewalk in the shopping center. The unloaded truck then veered into the northbound lane of South Eagle Road, driving over a Toyota Camry, "flattening it like a pancake," said Newtown Police Sgt. Stephen Meyers.

The truck then jumped a curb and plowed into the First Union Bank, narrowly avoiding a car that was pulling into the drive-through. None of the eight people inside the bank was hurt, although one customer entering the bank fainted, said police.

"When you went into the bank, all you could see was trampled wall and ceiling," said one witness. "The only thing I could make out was a toilet. I can't imagine what would have been if the truck was full."

Teresa Concepcion, 36, of Mahogany Walk, the driver of the Camry, received injuries to her head and torso. She was listed in serious condition last night at St. Mary Medical Center in Middletown, according to a nursing supervisor. Her injuries were not life-threatening, said police.

Truck driver Steven S. Vile Sr., 39, of the 1800 block of Lincoln Street, Bristol Township, was being treated at St. Mary Medical Center in Middletown for minor injuries. He was in fair condition last night, the nursing supervisor said.

Police would not say what caused the accident and many details were still sketchy, including who had the green light at the intersection. Police did say Eagle Road is closed to truck traffic unless the driver is making a delivery. Truckers at the scene said the company does a lot of the sewer installations for developments throughout the township. The speed limit on the road is 35 mph.

"We know how it took place," said Meyers. "But we don't know what caused it."

The owner of CVA Inc., in Falls, which owns the truck, could not be reached for comment, although police said a manager for the company had been at the scene. Police also said they have interviewed Vile, who is cooperating.

"I heard a crunching sound and something like a car rolling over," said a roofer who was working about a quarter mile from the scene, but wouldn't give his name. "But I didn't hear anything like brakes screeching."

However, police said it was still unclear whether any of the skid marks at the scene were the result of the truck driver trying to brake.

Work continued throughout the day to shore up the wall of the bank around the truck so the vehicle could be removed. From the road, all that was visible was its tailgate.

"We heard a noise coming from this direction," said one witness as she pointed at the accident scene. "And by the time I got there, all I could see was the stone truck going through the building."

Several municipalities are assisting in the investigation, including state police and the Public Utility Commission, which oversees truck inspections. Investigators are using videotape from the accident scene, accounts from at least a dozen witnesses and aerial shots taken from a police helicopter. The truck has been impounded. Lt. Gordon Beck of Newtown Township is heading the investigation.

More than 50 volunteers from Newtown Ambulance, Newtown Fire Association, Middletown Emergency Squad, Yardley-Makefield Fire Co., Langhorne-Middletown Fire Co. and Northampton Fire Co. responded to the call.

Louise Kaplan of Newtown Borough snapped her own photos of the accident. Had this happened on a Saturday morning, she said, a lot more people would have been hurt.

"The customers line up outside the bank before it opens on Saturday," she said, looking up at the hill on Eagle Road where the truck had come from. "There's nothing to stop you when you're coming down that hill."

Reprinted with permission from the Bucks County Courier Times.

INTERNET EXERCISES

Many fire departments put incident reports and press releases online; these can be used as the basis for newswriting exercises. Here are a few examples:

Sacramento Fire Department   **http://www.cityofsacramento.org/fire/**

Fort Wayne, Ind., Fire Department   **http://www.fwfd.org/**

Grand Junction, Co., Fire Department   **http://www.gjcity.org/ CityDeptWebPages/FireDepartment/PublicEducation/PressRelease.htm**

Madison, Wi., Fire Department   **http://www.ci.madison.wi.us/fire/department_ news/fire_department_news.htm**

Double Oak, Texas, Fire Department   **http://www.dovfd.org/**

BEYOND THE CLASSROOM

Visit a local fire department headquarters and interview an official there about a major fire or rescue situation they've handled recently. Write a story.

6

Stormy Weather and Natural Disasters

*r*eporters who are experienced at covering storms and natural disasters—blizzards, earthquakes, hurricanes, tornadoes, floods, volcanoes, forest fires and so on—know there are two kinds of information they need to get for every story. The first is hard, official facts about the number of casualties, the extent of property damage, and the status of the search and rescue, recovery, or rebuilding efforts. The second is the human side of the story—firsthand accounts of what happened from people who lived through it, from people who have lost homes or loved ones, and from people who responded heroically to help their neighbors in a moment of absolute need.

Both kinds of information are crucial. The story that is chock-full of colorful quotes but lacking in basic information leaves a reader frustrated and bewildered. The fact-packed article that has no real human voices in it can leave a reader cold. And at the scene of a natural disaster, when basic amenities that we take for granted, such as roads, bridges, electric power or a sense of civil order, are swept away, getting such information can be difficult indeed.

Reporters covering such stories must quickly sort out rumors and secondhand stories from hard facts. It's vital to find an official, reliable source of information, whether it's police, fire officials or civil defense personnel. Likewise, reporters arriving at the scene of a devastated area only to encounter a police roadblock must be creative in finding ways to get past such barriers to reach the people who are really being affected by the disaster at hand. In other words, the reporter covering a natural disaster must find order in the chaos. He must take an extraordinarily confusing situation and make it clear and understandable for his readers.

"You have to make sure you're really clear-headed at these kinds of things," says Stephen Manning, an Associated Press correspondent who has covered several tornadoes. "It's easy to get swept up and miss important things. If you walk through a town that's been blown apart, you can't stand around and gawk," he adds. "You have to write down what you're seeing. You have to talk to people."

It's also necessary to maintain a certain professional reserve while covering such stories. The reporter covering an earthquake or tornado may see dead bodies for the first time in his life. He may encounter distraught, grief-stricken victims of what has happened. He may find it overwhelming. But, Manning says, "you have to detach yourself from what's going on around you and look at it as an outsider. You have to keep your wits about you." After all, a distraught reporter does no one any good. It's the reporter's job to provide solid, reliable information in a time of crisis.

QUICK TIPS

- Rely on official sources for hard information, such as the number of casualties, the extent of damage and the status of any search and/or rescue operations.
- Be wary of rumors, speculation and information from people not affiliated with officials handling the response to the disaster.
- Interview real people affected by the event for color and quotes. These are the people who will bring this story to life for your readers.

exercise one

Hurricane Bonnie has hit Barco, a small coastal town in North Carolina. Write a story based on your notes and observations from the scene. Deadline: 30 minutes.

The storm is bearing down on the Carolina coast and the entire town has been evacuated. High winds have knocked out power to the town and a storm surge has flooded roads everywhere. Driving through the streets that are still passable there are trees flattened and sparks flying from downed power lines. The winds ripped the roof off St. Mary's Hospital and dozens of patients had to be evacuated to St. Marks, the town's other main hospital. Cops and civil defense people are about the only people on the streets, except for 83-year-old Jake Wilson, who's standing on the porch of his tiny bungalow. Wilson is a widower who has decided to sit out the storm. He says: "I've seen these storms come and go for years and I've always survived. I didn't move then, I ain't moving now." The police say that one person, a 12-year-old child, was killed when a tree fell on her house. Three other people have been injured in the storm so far. The police don't have any names yet.

exercise two

You're a reporter for the Centurion, the student newspaper at Bucks County Community College in Newtown, Pa. Write a story for tomorrow's paper based on the following information. Deadline: 40 minutes.

On Monday morning the campus was hit by a surprise snowstorm. Weather forecasters predicted only 4 inches of snow. This morning it was only raining. But by midday heavy snow and ice were falling, so college officials closed the campus at noon. Now several thousand students are all trying to drive off the commuter campus at once. Vehicles are sliding all over roads as they slowly inch their way along. Warren Horrocks, the college's director of Security and Safety, says he saw "vehicles slipping and sliding all over the roads." Horrocks says there were several accidents on campus, though none serious. He said he saw one car that had slipped off the road into a field and got stuck. He also saw many people helping push cars across the roads and out of the large piles of snow.

By late afternoon the National Weather Service says 10 inches have been dumped on the area. You call Matt Kerr, president of the college's student government, at home. He says, "It was horrible. I have a Jeep with four-wheel drive and I was sliding all over the place." Kerr says the storm seemed to take snowplow crews by surprise. "I expected the road crews to be out but they weren't. . . . They didn't plow, they didn't salt."

exercise three

Based on the following information, write a story about the high winds and rain that hit Jefferson County, Mo., this afternoon. Deadline: one hour.

National Weather Service officials say the storms produced either straight-line winds or a tornado that moved through the Heads Creek valley along Highway MM in House Springs. The storms also hit pockets of St. Charles County but skipped the city of St. Louis, leaving only light rain. In Illinois, the Weather Service reported the storms produced only light rain in the Metro East area before moving south. No one was injured, but the storms toppled dozens of trees and snapped limbs and utility poles. A lightning strike cut off service to the Jefferson County Emergency Dispatch Center in House Springs for about 10 minutes until authorities activated a backup system. Crews from AmerenUE planned to work through the night tonight if necessary to restore service to about 17,650 customers who lost power. In Jefferson City, the storms knocked out electricity for up to 45 minutes at several state buildings. About 8,000 customers lost power in Wentzville, where winds up to 55 miles per hour knocked down trees, ripped away roofs and snapped telephone poles. Residents in Chesterfield and Wildwood also experienced power outages. The storms forced the Wentzville police department, fire stations and hospitals to operate on emergency power generators. At Interstate 70 and Pearce Boulevard, winds blew away the roof of a carwash. The debris landed about 30 yards away on Norfolk and Southern railroad tracks. Railroad officials briefly shut down the tracks to clear the debris. Workers closed Highway Z for several hours to clear trees that covered the road.

You interview Stacy Mann, who says it sent a chill down her spine when she saw a utility pole outside her house snapped in two, with the top half still dangling from the wires. Mann's nephew, Andy Mann, 17, was electrocuted in January when his Jeep Wrangler slid on icy pavement and struck a utility pole following a snowstorm near his house in High Ridge. Stacy, her husband, Bob, and their daughter, Samantha, 11, rode out the storms in the basement of their house in the 6000 block of Parkridge Drive in House Springs. "At first it didn't seem that bad," Mann says. "But when I looked out again, you couldn't even see."

Steve Davis, chief of the High Ridge Fire Protection District, says he was following his crew back from an emergency call around 3 p.m. when rain blowing horizontally across Highway 30 forced them to pull over to the side of the road. "The car was just rocking," Davis says.

exercise four

Write a story based on the following information. Deadline: one hour.

You're a reporter for the Houston bureau of The Associated Press. It's Sunday, and you're writing an update on Tropical Storm Allison, which started hitting southeast Texas Friday afternoon with torrential rains and floods. Houston Mayor Lee Brown held a press conference today in which he estimated that 5,000 homes and businesses have been damaged by the storm. Tax assessor Paul Bettencourt, also at the press conference, says at least 10,000 homes are believed damaged in Harris County. "Our estimate of $100 million in home damage could increase dramatically," Bettencourt says. "It could be a quarter-billion dollars." Asked about the damage estimate, Brown says, "If I were to give a guess . . . it would top $1 billion. That would be a guess, but it would suggest we have had a serious problem." Floodwaters are now receding in most areas. Skies are cloudy today and forecasts are for little or no additional rain. Most of the heavier rain has moved to the east into Louisiana, where at least one fatality has been reported. At his press conference, Brown says 12 deaths from the storm have been confirmed in Texas. Also today, an investigator at the Harris County medical examiner's office says that most of the victims were presumed drowned but two or three are believed to have been electrocuted. Officials say they fear the death toll could rise. Meanwhile, some people are still being rescued from the floodwaters. Some residents, primarily on Houston's east side, had to be rescued from their homes today by National Guard troops in 5-ton trucks who arrived after Gov. Rick Perry declared a 28-county area disaster area. President Bush yesterday declared the area a federal disaster area. At the Harris County Jail, which is adjacent to Buffalo Bayou in downtown Houston, 3,000 inmates had to be moved to other lockups when floods knocked out water and electric service. "The inmates have been cooperative," prison spokesman Bob Van Pelt tells you.

Real
REPORTER: Stephen Manning

Stephen Manning was sitting down to dinner on the evening of April 28, 2002, when he got a call. It was the Baltimore bureau of The Associated Press. "They were getting information that people in La Plata were trapped in structures and that a tornado had gone through," Manning recalls. "They were calling the cops and the cops couldn't talk. That usually means something's going on." Something was. A monster tornado had torn through the heart of La Plata, a town of about 6,000 people in Maryland. Damage appeared to be extensive, and there were likely casualties. Manning's dinner would have to wait. A big story was breaking, and he had to be there.

Manning is an AP correspondent, a title given more senior reporters in the wire service. AP correspondents are responsible for covering large areas of a state on their own. Manning covers Montgomery, Prince Georges and Charles counties in Maryland—an area that contains roughly a third of the state's population.

Manning hit the road for the hour-long drive to La Plata. He arrived to a scene of devastation. The twister had cut a swath through the center of the town's business district, leveling shops and tearing up streets. Police were turning people away from the most badly damaged areas, but as a reporter Manning had to get past the police barricade.

"It was incredibly chaotic," he says. "I had to sweet-talk my way into the scene. I was able to get past the barricade and just started walking through the town. It was pitch black, all the power was out. I kept tripping over power lines. The whole business section was just gone. What was once a Kentucky Fried Chicken was just two bricks high. Homes and businesses were ripped apart. I started grabbing people and interviewing them," he adds. "That's when you get your best stuff, when it's chaotic and you can get people's reactions to that. And those are the times you can get firefighters or cops at the scene to talk to you, before they get organized and start referring you to a PR person."

Back at the Baltimore bureau, reporters were working the phones, trying to get information from police and fire officials. But as any reporter will tell you, only so much information can be gotten in a phone interview. On a big story, a reporter needs to be at the scene. Getting reliable information at the scene of a disaster like a tornado, however, is tricky. And as a reporter for the wire service, Manning didn't have minutes or hours until his deadline. His deadline was immediate.

The AP supplies news to newspapers and broadcast outlets across the country and around the world. In many ways, the AP is the "first alert" system of journalism, letting editors and producers know a big story is coming. Since everyone relies on the AP for breaking news, AP reporters face a deadline every minute.

With news like the La Plata tornado, there was no time for Manning to sit down and write a complete story on his laptop, then send it to the Baltimore bureau. Indeed, reporters at the bureau had already sent a barebones story out on the wire. Instead, he had to gather information as quickly as he could, and phone it in to a reporter back in Baltimore. The bureau reporter would insert Manning's new information into the story, then send it out on the wire in what's known in the AP as a "writethru." A writethru simply means that the story is being updated. On a big event like a tornado, the story out on the AP wire can go through a dozen or more writethrus.

"With the AP your deadline is now. You have to get information out as fast as you can," Manning says. "A lot of other news organizations use your material as a guide. Broadcast outlets use it live. With that kind of situation you have to be really sure you're correct in what you're reporting. You have to get the information really nailed down." Manning interviewed as many people as he could on the streets, getting plenty of colorful quotes and firsthand accounts of the story. But he knew he also had to get official information on the basics—the number of injured and dead, the extent of the damage, the status of the rescue and cleanup operation. So he made his way to the local courthouse, where a command center had been set up for police, fire and rescue personnel.

"Once I got a good sense of the scene I made my way back to the command center. That becomes your best source of information," Manning says. "There they gave us periodic updates. First they told us one person was dead. Around 1 a.m. they told us a second person had died. There were a lot of injuries from flying debris." As the night wore on, the command center updates became less frequent. So Manning headed to a nearby high school that was serving as a shelter for people forced out of their homes. He found plenty of people to interview.

"You should get that kind of color into your story," Manning says. "It's important to have official information, but you also want to paint a picture of the scene. You want to convey to your readers what this looks like and how it affects people. You can say in your story that two people died, but if you talk to someone who knew them, it's a lot more powerful."

Often, Manning says, "the things that make a story really rich are minor details that you might not notice. It can seem minor but be emblematic of the larger situation." For example, he spied an unrecognizable pile of rubble. Residents told him it had been a Kentucky Fried Chicken. "That was an interesting detail," he says. "It was something that everyone knew and recognized, and it just wasn't there any more."

Manning kept reporting the story through the night and into the next day. He tried to catch a catnap or two in his car, but marathon shifts are the rule for reporters covering a story like this. "I got there around 9 or 10 at night, and was there until 3 p.m. the next day," he recalls. "You drink a lot of coffee, and at a certain point you get used to it. There's the adrenaline rush of it. It's exciting. But when you've been up a long time it's easy to get a little loose with the facts. You have to pay very close attention to what you're reporting when you're tired."

The death toll from the La Plata tornado eventually reached five; nearly 100 people were injured. Manning, working with the Baltimore AP bureau, did more than a dozen writethrus on the story.

Manning graduated with a degree in history from Haverford College in 1996. After stints with a college magazine and public radio, he started with the AP as a reporter in the Baltimore bureau. He became a correspondent in 2000. He says working at the AP is different in several ways from working at a local paper. For one thing, your articles aren't limited to one publication—they can be sent around the world. Also, since AP bureaus tend to be small, most AP reporters don't have a specific beat. They cover anything and everything.

"At the AP you need to be able to pick up things very quickly," he explains. "You should be able to take something you're not familiar with and digest it fast." Digest it fast, and write it even faster, he adds. "Fast writing is something you have to get used to at the AP," Manning says. "AP stories tend to be a little shorter, and often a little more concise, than newspaper stories. You get used to that style of writing." Needless to say, the ability to write clear, concise sentences is all-important. To ensure that its reporters can do this, anyone applying for an AP reporting job must take a writing test.

"It's not the easiest life," Manning says. "There are crazy shifts, weekends, late nights. But then again, you can get incredibly wide exposure, and you can cover really important issues." Below is Manning's story about the La Plata tornado.

La PLATA, Md. (AP) A tornado ripped through southern Maryland, killing three people, injuring nearly 100, shearing off homes at their foundations and snapping off treetops.

Two people were killed Sunday in La Plata. One victim was identified as William G. Erickson Jr., who was killed when his house collapsed, said Nina Voehl, a spokeswoman for Charles County.

His wife, Susan, escaped from the house, Voehl said. She was in serious but stable condition Monday at Prince George's Hospital Center in Cheverly.

A neighbor, Laura Silk, said the Ericksons were visiting their home, which was under construction. Silk said the house was about 80 percent complete.

The tornado leveled Silk's house. She saw it coming and ran upstairs to get her husband and children. The family hid under a mattress in the basement.

"It was like thinking you were going to die every second," Silk said. "I was in shock, I was crying."

A second person died at U.S. 301 and Maryland Route 6 in Charles County, said Jack Haly, a spokesman for the Maryland Emergency Management Agency. He did not have any further information.

A tornado also reportedly touched down in Calvert County, killing Margaret Albey, 74, of Prince Frederick. Neighbors said her small, wood-frame home lay directly in the tornado's path.

"The house is gone. It's moved probably 80 yards down and into a ravine," said Sgt. Rick Thomas of the county sheriff's office. "They were in the house and trapped in the rubble."

Neighbors found Albey and her 77-year-old husband, George, huddled together underneath a couch. George Albey was in good condition Monday at Washington Hospital Center.

A tornado also was reported on the Eastern Shore, but there were no injuries.

Gov. Parris Glendening declared a state of emergency for Charles and Calvert counties. That allowed the state to request the help of the National Guard, which sent troops to the area.

Lt. Gov. Kathleen Kennedy Townsend said the state contacted the Federal Emergency Management Agency about whether Maryland should apply for a disaster declaration.

"Anything we can do, we stand ready to help," Townsend said Monday as she visited a shelter at Thomas Stone High School in Waldorf.

Jack Cahalan, a spokesman with the Maryland Emergency Management Administration, said Monday that 93 people were injured, mostly in La Plata.

National Weather Service meteorologists visited the area Monday to determine the strength of the storm and the extent of the damage. Meteorologist James Travers said the tornado was probably as severe as one that hit the same area in 1926, killing 13 children.

The tornado hit La Plata about 7 p.m. Sunday and damaged at least a 10-mile stretch from the town of about 6,500 to Hughesville in Charles County.

Cahalan said 81 people had minor to serious injuries from the tornado. Another 12 were critically injured and sent to Washington-area hospitals, Cahalan said.

Part of Archbishop Neale Elementary School was leveled.

"It's awful," said Dennis Albrecht, who sends his three kids to the school. "I don't know what we're going to do for this school year."

People drove and wandered around La Plata's streets Monday, gawking at the damage. Some took photos and some cried as they looked over destroyed buildings. Around a section of damaged office buildings, workers sorted through files scattered outside.

In Calvert County, the Red Cross said four homes were destroyed, three had moderate damage and 16 homes sustained minor damage. The Red Cross helped 11 families find motel rooms.

In Dorchester County, a barn and a home were demolished and trees and telephone wires were uprooted. A family of four was not at home when the residence was destroyed.

"It's just like someone sucked it up with a vacuum cleaner," said Capt. James Phillips, chief deputy of the sheriff's department.

In Charles County, many of the injured were treated at Civista Medical Center in La Plata, said CEO Chris Stefanides.

"They're banged up and shocked, and they're frightened," Stefanides said. "I don't think they've ever really seen anything like this before."

Shawn Murphy, who was delivering pizzas in La Plata when the tornado hit, described the funnel cloud as about 20 feet wide.

"It just started tearing up everything," Murphy said.

Charles County Sheriff Fred Davis said rescuers extracted several people from a collapsed building. He did not know their conditions.

Davis said rescue workers went from home to home in La Plata, searching through rubble for people who might still be trapped.

Cahalan said power was knocked out to as many as 17,000 customers. By 4 a.m., he said power was still out for about 4,500 customers. Power lines were down on roads.

All public schools in Charles County were closed Monday, said Katie O'Malley-Simpson, a spokeswoman for county schools. South Dorchester School also was closed Monday because of debris on roads, and school bus service for the southern part of the county was canceled.

Reprinted with permission of The Associated Press.

INTERNET EXERCISES

The National Oceanic and Atmospheric Web site has a wealth of weather- and environment-related information that can be used to generate lots of stories. The agency's home page is at **http://www.noaa.gov/**. NOAA even has a special page set up for reporters with ideas for stories about the weather. That page can be found at **http://www.publicaffairs. noaa.gov/storyideas.html**.

The Federal Emergency Management Agency, or FEMA, coordinates the federal government's response to very serious natural disasters. You can find its Web site at **http://www.fema.gov**.

BEYOND THE CLASSROOM

- Check the "Active Disasters" section of the FEMA Web site. Look for disasters FEMA is currently handling. Interview a FEMA official about the disaster and what the agency is doing in response. Write a story.

- Check the "news releases" section. Find a release dealing with FEMA's response to a disaster nearest to where you live. Read the press release, interview a FEMA official about the response and write a story.

- Log onto the NOAA Web site. Find a NOAA news release that pertains to your area of the country. Read the release, then contact a NOAA expert and interview him or her for more information. For example, if you live on the East Coast, you might write about the coming hurricane season, and experts' predictions of how severe it will be. Use the news release and your interview to write an article.

chapter seven

Speeches and Press Conferences

*a*t first glance, a speech or a press conference must seem like the easiest kind of story a reporter covers. After all, the reporter doesn't have to track down an elusive source or convince a reluctant interviewee to speak. The speaker is right there in front of her, talking openly and publicly. All she has to do is take notes, then write her story. Sometimes, reporters are given a prepared text of the speaker's remarks, making even note-taking unnecessary. What could be easier?

In fact, speeches or press conferences can be tough assignments. There's the challenge of capturing the speaker's quotes. Getting an exact quote down on paper can be difficult, especially when a speaker is talking quickly. Novice reporters often try to take down everything a speaker says, which is usually an exercise in futility. It's all but impossible to get every quote from, say, a 30-minute speech. The larger question is, should a reporter even try to get every quote? The answer is an emphatic no. Reporters are journalists, not stenographers. The experienced reporter knows that even when he's covering a long speech or press conference, he's only likely to use a few direct quotes in his story. Remember, news articles are generally short, and most of the time there simply isn't room for a long string of quotes. Instead, experienced reporters listen for the good quote. That's the one they jot down in their notes for possible use in their article.

GETTING THE "GOOD" QUOTE

But what makes a *good* quote? Generally speaking, it's the quote that brings the speaker, and his words, to life. A good quote can be colorful or dramatic, provocative or disturbing, but it should always get the reader's attention.

Consider the following two quotes:

We will use U.S. military force in an appropriate and decisive manner.

When I take action, I'm not going to fire a $2 million missile at a $10 empty tent and hit a camel in the butt. It's going to be decisive.

The first quote was made up by the author. The second quote comes from President George W. Bush, speaking to a group of senators two days after the terrorist attacks on the World Trade Center and the Pentagon. Both basically say the same thing, but which is the better quote? The second one, of course. The first one is dry, restrained and academic-sounding. The second is colorful, funny and descriptive. It manages, in just a few words, to paint a picture in the reader's mind (an odd picture, no doubt), and to give the reader a glimpse of the personality of the speaker. The president's Texas upbringing and his natural penchant for humor all come through in that quote. Not every quote will be that good. But in general, if a quote is colorful, thought-provoking, dramatic or descriptive, chances are it's a quote worth using.

Reporters covering speeches and press conferences must also be mindful of the need to *structure* their stories. That means deciding what goes into the lead of the story, what goes in the middle, and what comes at the bottom. The beginning reporter is often tempted to cover a speech chronologically, so that what the speaker says at the start of his talk automatically becomes the lead, and what he says in his closing remarks becomes the story's final paragraph. But speeches usually aren't organized like news articles. The speaker won't necessarily make his most important remarks in his first paragraph. Sometimes the most interesting thing said in a speech will come at the very end. Instead of transcribing a speech like a stenographer, from start to finish, the reporter must find the lead of the story. In other words, she must listen to the speech, take notes, decide what's most important and interesting about the speech and make that her lead.

This rule is especially important in covering press conferences, which tend to be much more chaotic and less organized than speeches. Again, the reporter uses news judgment, not chronology, to decide what goes at the beginning, middle and end of the story. The seasoned reporter knows he is under no obligation to cover events like these chronologically; he views the speech or press conference as raw material to be shaped, as he sees fit, into a coherent, well-written news story.

exercise one

Write a story based on the following information. Deadline: 30 minutes.

You're a reporter for the Collegian, the Centerville State College student newspaper. The college is holding a ribbon-cutting ceremony for the opening of two high-tech computer labs on campus. A crowd of about 50 students and faculty are present for the event. College President Jane Larsen is there to make some brief remarks. These are your notes from her talk:

"We're thrilled to be opening these new computer labs. These state-of-the-art classrooms will enable students to do word processing, access the Internet and create Web pages. It's this kind of innovation that's bringing Centerville State College into the 21st century.

"We'd especially like to thank the state and federal government for the money that made the creation of these labs possible. Without a $50,000 grant from the state Department of Education, and additional money from the federal government, we would never have been able to complete these labs.

"Unfortunately, it appears as if state funding for higher education is drying up. With the economy slowing and tax revenues down, we've recently learned that Centerville State College will receive about 5 percent less in state funding next year. That drop in funding will have to be made up by an increase in tuition. I'm sorry to say that Centerville State College tuition will increase 5 percent beginning next fall."

Many in the crowd start to boo, and Larsen quickly leaves. As you return to the newsroom to write your story, you recall that full-time tuition at the college is about $4,000.

exercise two

Write a story based on the following information. Deadline: 40 minutes.

The Centerville Chamber of Commerce is holding its monthly luncheon at the Hotel Luxe. The guest speaker today is Dr. Wiley Perkins, a cardiologist and expert on physical fitness from nearby Farber General Hospital. The title of Perkins' talk is "The Facts About Fad Diets." Perkins himself is a fit and trim 62-year-old. About 100 area business men and women are present for his talk. Here are your notes from his speech:

"More and more Americans are overweight. In fact, a recent poll found that that 80 percent of people older than 25 are overweight. That's up from 58 percent in 1983. Yet while Americans are getting rounder and softer around the middle, they're turning not to tried-and-true methods of weight loss, but to fad diets that often do more harm than good. There's the juice diet, the bacon diet, the banana diet, the water diet—the list goes on and on.

"Many of these diets leave dieters dehydrated, undernourished and weak. Some leave them with arteries more clogged than they were before. Folks, I'm here to tell you there's a better way.

"The best way—the only way—to shed weight is to cut your caloric intake while increasing your energy expenditure. In other words, eat less, exercise more. And the only safe way to do this is gradually, over time. A crash diet that promises you'll lose 10 pounds in a week not only won't work, it could hurt you.

"I myself run three miles a day and limit myself to a 2,000-calorie-a-day diet. But you don't have to run. New studies are finding that even vigorous walking, combined with a cut in calories, can aid weight loss."

Perkins suddenly stops speaking, grabs his chest and collapses at the podium. Several people gather around him, and paramedics are called. He's taken to Farber General Hospital. The nursing supervisor says in a phone call there a short while later that he died of a heart attack in the ambulance.

exercise three

Write a story based on the following information. Deadline: 45 minutes.

Phil Longwood, owner of a local carpet store, is running for mayor of Centerville, his first run for public office. He holds a press conference in front of City Hall to announce his plan to cut city income taxes. Here are your notes from the press conference, including questions from assembled reporters.

"I'm announcing today that, should I be elected mayor of the great city of Centerville, I plan to cut city income taxes 5 percent. This much-needed measure will help attract more businesses to the city. Right now we're driving businesses and corporations out of the city with our ridiculously high taxes. We need to attract new businesses to stimulate economic growth. As a small businessman I have experience with this sort of thing. If we don't do this, the city will become an economic sinkhole."

Q: Mr. Longwood, how do you plan to pay for this tax cut?
Longwood: Uh, what do you mean?
Q: I mean, where will the money come from? If you're going to cut the income tax, won't you have to cut city services as well? What will you cut? Garbage collection? Money for the public schools? Maintenance of city parks?
Longwood: Uh, well, I don't expect to have to cut very much, because by attracting new business to the city, revenues will naturally increase.
Q: What do you mean by "not very much?"
Longwood: Well, just what I said. Not very much.
Q: How much is not very much?
Longwood: I'm not prepared to say at this point.
Q: What services do you plan to cut "not very much?"
Longwood: I haven't decided yet.
Q: Mr. Longwood, even if your plan does attract new business to the city, and even if that does mean more revenue for the city, won't that take years to happen? Where will the city come up with the money in the meantime?
Longwood: Uh, I'm not sure about that.

At this point Longwood, who is by now very red in the face, yells, "You damn reporters just want to twist everything around and make it negative." He storms off the podium and is whisked away by his handlers.

exercise four

Write a story based on the following information. Deadline: 45 minutes.

It's several days after carpet-store-owner-turned-mayoral-candidate Phil Longwood held his press conference on cutting the city's income tax. He's holding another press conference, this time in front of his suburban home. A group of reporters have gathered to listen. Here are your notes:

"Several days ago I offered up a proposal that I believed would dramatically enhance the economic future of this city. It was and is my belief that unless Centerville cuts taxes and attracts new business and investment, this city will become an economic wasteland.

"Employment in Centerville has dropped every year for the last five years. Fewer new jobs are being created in the city now than at any time in the last decade. As you all know, two big firms have left the city in recent years, and others are considering doing the same thing. I believe this is due to a city income tax that stifles business growth and expansion.

"However, instead of getting a fair hearing, my proposal to cut taxes was met with criticism and derision. The press lambasted it and my political opponents skewered it. People who have little or no business experience took me to task for what they said was a bad plan, a stupid plan. But as a small businessman I'm here to tell the city that tax relief is desperately needed. I may be a lone voice in the wilderness on this issue, but I will continue to speak out, because I love this city. I will continue to fight the good fight.

"Unfortunately, however, I won't be doing so as a candidate for mayor. This campaign and the criticism I've received have been very hard on my family—my wife, Vera, and my two daughters, Sally and Erica. It's been heartbreaking for them to see me attacked in the local media like this. So, after a long talk with my wife, I've decided to drop out of the race for mayor. I do so with great hesitation, because as I said I love this city and want to see it grow. But the political

arena just isn't for me. As I said, I will continue to make my voice heard. I will fight my battles in other ways. But for now, I'm taking my family on vacation."

Longwood retreats back into his house, taking no questions from reporters.

exercise five

What follows is the transcript of a speech given by U.S. Rep. Jim Greenwood, who represents Bucks County, Pa. The speech was given at a VFW post in Levittown. Write a story based on his speech, using the Internet to research any historical background you might need. Deadline: one hour.

Good morning ladies and gentlemen, and thank you for being here to help the commissioners and me to honor the American heroes of D-Day. We are grateful to the VFW Post for hosting this special ceremony. Most especially, I want to thank the D-Day veterans, as it is your victory that we celebrate. You are living monuments of arguably the greatest invasion in world history.

With the benefit of hindsight and with the knowledge that the Normandy Invasion was an enormous success, many of us may not comprehend just how risky the operation was. The architects of the D-Day invasions—people like Winston Churchill and Dwight Eisenhower—understood the enormous gamble they were taking, which is why Churchill dubbed the mission "Operation Overlord": it was so ambitious in size and objective that, once begun, there was no turning back.

The Allies assembled a tremendous armada of five thousand, three hundred thirty-three (5,333) ships carrying an invasion force of approximately one hundred seventy-five thousand (175,000) men. To put this in perspective, consider our more recent war in Afghanistan: by May of this year—nearly eight months after the terrorist attacks of September 11—the total number of American personnel in Afghanistan totaled six thousand (6,000) troops, less than 3 percent of the D-Day invasion force.

For D-Day's mammoth operation to succeed, overwhelming challenges would need to

be overcome. First, the Allies had to outfox German intelligence and keep the details of the invasion a secret. The Germans knew that an attack was coming, but they did not know where or when it would come. Imagine: mobilizing 5,000 ships and 175,000 men across an ocean, all the while keeping your arrival a surprise. In all likelihood, such a feat will never again be replicated.

Most of the Allied soldiers, in fact, did not know their destination until they were en route to Normandy through the English Channel. The Channel, a dangerously unpredictable body of water, posed another challenge to the thousands of ships. The tumultuous rides caused seasickness in many of these men, men who were simultaneoulsly trying to brace themselves as they prepared for battle.

Some troops, such as the 4th Infantry Division, were forced to spend an extra day at sea because the ocean was too rough for the landing. Bottled like sardines in a can, the restless crew was forced to wait, as one private described, in a "stench of vomit." And the waiting, the anticipation, must have been maddening. While an incredible tempest of fear and eagerness and adreneline filled the hearts of every passenger, the soldiers had no choice but to wait it out. Minutes seemed like hours, and hours felt like lifetimes.

Eventually, the hour arrived. The Allied troops neared the landing point greeted by the deafening sounds of bombardments from the German guns and from the firing of their own ships. It was painfully loud, and terrifying. Even General Omar Bradley said that he had "never heard anything like it" in his entire life.

At 6:31 a.m., June 5, 1944, the first landing began at Utah Beach. As for the events of the next few hours, most of us can only try to comprehend what our brave men experienced. The beaches themselves were bristling with traps. Anticipating the attack, German field marshal Erwin Rommel had filled the beaches with mines, barbed wire, and tank traps. By the time the Allies landed, there were roughly half a million of these obstacles in place, waiting to ensnare the invaders.

Even more daunting were the Germans themselves: eighty thousand (80,000) troops and one panzer division that showered the Allies with incessant firepower. The Germans had perched their long-range guns in high, well-fortified positions on the beach. In fact, from their superior vantage point, the German gunners could see the Allied ships through the cloud cover before the ships could see the guns. Yet, our men stormed the hazardous beaches through the mines, the wire, the gun fire and the explosions.

The best visual re-creation we have into these horrible moments is the opening scene of the movie "Saving Private Ryan." Director Steven Speilberg overwhelms us with the blood and confusion that surrounded the Americans. The film helps us to begin to understand how difficult it must have been to function amidst such chaos. It shows what it was like to have your buddy standing beside you one minute and then, right before your eyes, to see him taken away forever. We see how the cries of the wounded would long remain unanswered, because few doctors accompanied the first wave.

In spite of all the horror, the Allies did not yield. They did not turn back. Instead, they dove head first into a thicket of danger. They overcame the Germans, they overcame their fears, and they did their job.

The Allied commanders, leaders like Eisenhower and Churchill, designed Operation Overlord and made the bold decision to invade. But it was the soldiers like you who made the invasion work and D-Day a day for all ages. You trained vigorously. You made a treacherous journey to a foreign land, without knowing where you were going, and without the promise of ever returning home. You risked everything. And you did your job.

You, veterans of Normandy, are living history. We are grateful for what you have done for us, and grateful for this chance to honor you. For as columnist Bob Greene of the Chicago Tribune has said: "They are leaving us now, the men and women of these war years; soon we, their children, will be all alone in the world they saved for us." As we were painfully and cruelly reminded on 9-11, there is much evil and danger in this world, a world that needs saving again. As we face this challenge together, we take this day to remember you, Normandy veterans, and the great feats of which Americans are capable. Guided by your example, strengthened by the legacy of sacrifice and courage that you have given us, we will roll on. We salute you, we thank you, and we ask that God Bless America.

Write a story based on this Sept. 28, 2002, radio address by President George W. Bush. Deadline: one hour.

Good morning. On Thursday, I met with Democratic and Republican members of Congress to discuss the threat posed by the Iraqi regime. The security of our country is the commitment of both political parties, and the responsibility of both the president and the Congress. We are united in our determination to confront this urgent threat to America.

We're moving toward a strong resolution authorizing the use of force, if necessary, to defend our national security interests against the threat posed by Saddam Hussein. And by passing this resolution we will send a clear message to the world community and to the Iraqi regime the demands of the United Nations Security Council must be followed: the Iraqi dictator must be disarmed. These requirements will be met, or they will be enforced.

The danger to our country is grave and it is growing. The Iraqi regime possesses biological and chemical weapons, is rebuilding the facilities to make more and, according to the British government, could launch a biological or chemical attack in as little as 45 minutes after the order is given. The regime has long-standing and continuing ties to terrorist groups, and there are al Qaeda terrorists inside Iraq. This regime is seeking a nuclear bomb, and with fissile material could build one within a year.

Iraq has already used weapons of mass death against another country and against its own citizens. The Iraqi regime practices the rape of women as a method of intimidation, and the torture of dissenters and their children. And for more than a decade, that regime has answered Security Council resolutions with defiance and bad faith and deception.

We know that the Iraqi regime is led by a dangerous and brutal man. We know he is actively seeking the destructive technologies to match his hatred. And we know that he must be stopped. The dangers we face will only worsen from month to month and year to year. To ignore these threats is to encourage them—and when they have fully materialized, it may be too late to protect ourselves and our allies. By then, the Iraqi dictator will have had the means to terrorize and dominate the region, and each passing day could be the one on which the Iraqi regime gives anthrax or VX nerve gas or someday a nuclear weapon to a terrorist group.

We refuse to live in this future of fear. We are determined to build a future of security and peace for ourselves and for the world. The members of Congress from both political parties with whom I met this week are committed to American leadership for the good of all nations. The resolution we are producing will be an instrument of that leadership.

I appreciate the spirit in which members of Congress are considering this vital issue. We're making progress, we are nearing agreement, and soon we will speak with one voice.

Thank you for listening.

exercise seven

What follows is a transcript of a speech President George W. Bush gave at Ellis Island, N.Y., on Sept. 11, 2002. Write a story based on his speech. Deadline: one hour.

Good evening. A long year has passed since enemies attacked our country. We've seen the images so many times they are seared on our souls, and remembering the horror, reliving the anguish, reimagining the terror, is hard—and painful.

For those who lost loved ones, it's been a year of sorrow, of empty places, of newborn children who will never know their fathers here on earth. For members of our military, it's been a year of sacrifice and service far from home. For all Americans, it has been a year of adjustment, of coming to terms with the difficult knowledge that our nation has determined enemies, and that we are not invulnerable to their attacks.

Yet, in the events that have challenged us, we have also seen the character that will deliver us. We have seen the greatness of America in airline passengers who defied their hijackers and ran a plane into the ground to spare the lives of others. We've seen the greatness of America in rescuers who rushed up flights of stairs toward peril. And we continue to see the greatness of America in the care and compassion our citizens show to each other.

September 11, 2001 will always be a fixed point in the life of America. The loss of so many lives left us to examine our own. Each of us was reminded that we are here only for a time, and these counted days should be filled with things that last and matter: love for our families, love for our neighbors, and for our country; gratitude for life and to the Giver of life.

We resolved a year ago to honor every last person lost. We owe them remembrance and we owe them more. We owe them, and their children, and our own, the most enduring monument we can build: a world of liberty and security made possible by the way America leads, and by the way Americans lead our lives.

The attack on our nation was also an attack on the ideals that make us a nation. Our deepest national conviction is that every life is precious, because every life is the gift of a Creator who intended us to live in liberty and equality. More than anything else, this separates us from the enemy we fight. We value every life; our enemies value none—not even the innocent, not even their own. And we seek the freedom and opportunity that give meaning and value to life.

There is a line in our time, and in every time, between those who believe all men are created equal, and those who believe that some men and women and children are expendable in the pursuit of power. There is a line in our time, and in every time, between the defenders of human liberty and those who seek to master the minds and souls of others. Our generation has now heard history's call, and we will answer it.

America has entered a great struggle that tests our strength, and even more our resolve. Our nation is patient and steadfast. We continue to pursue the terrorists in cities and camps and caves across the earth. We are joined by a great coalition of nations to rid the world of terror. And we will not allow any terrorist or tyrant to threaten civilization with weapons of mass murder. Now and in the future, Americans will live as free people, not in fear, and never at the mercy of any foreign plot or power.

This nation has defeated tyrants and liberated death camps, raised this lamp of liberty to every captive land. We have no intention of ignoring or appeasing history's latest gang of fanatics trying to murder their way to power. They are discovering, as others before them, the resolve of a great country and a great democracy. In the ruins of two towers, under a flag unfurled at the Pentagon, at the funerals of the lost, we have made a sacred promise to ourselves and to the world: we will not relent until justice is done and our nation is secure. What our enemies have begun, we will finish.

I believe there is a reason that history has matched this nation with this time. America strives to be tolerant and just. We respect the faith of Islam, even as we fight those whose actions defile that faith. We fight, not to impose our will, but to defend ourselves and extend the blessings of freedom.

We cannot know all that lies ahead. Yet, we do know that God had placed us together in this moment, to grieve together, to stand together, to serve each other and our country. And the duty we have been given—defending America and our freedom—is also a privilege we share.

We're prepared for this journey. And our prayer tonight is that God will see us through, and keep us worthy.

Tomorrow is September the 12th. A milestone is passed, and a mission goes on. Be confident. Our country is strong. And our cause is even larger than our country. Ours is the cause of human dignity; freedom guided by conscience and guarded by peace. This ideal of America is the hope of all mankind. That hope drew millions to this harbor. That hope still lights our way. And the light shines in the darkness. And the darkness will not overcome it.

May God bless America.

Real REPORTER: Jena Heath

For Jena Heath, newswriting is about telling a story. On Sept. 11, 2001, she had to tell the most important story of her career.

Heath, a White House correspondent for the Austin (Texas) American-Statesman newspaper and the Cox News Service, was assigned to tell readers what President George W. Bush had said and done in the hours immediately after terrorists attacked the World Trade Center and the Pentagon. The problem was, the president was in Florida. Heath was in Washington. The White House had been evacuated, cell phones were out, and in the chaos, no White House press briefings had been scheduled. So Heath did what any good reporter does. She reported.

Heath worked the phones as best she could, then hit the streets of the nation's capital to interview people for their reactions to the attacks. Late that afternoon, the White House press corps started to receive dispatches from pool reporters traveling with the president. (Pool reporters distribute their information to other reporters who are not at the scene of an event.) As she scanned those reports, Heath saw her story start to take shape. "I knew when I read the pool reports that the president had gone from a routine day of making a public appearance to having a top aide walk over and tell him the World Trade Center had been attacked," Heath says. "And this is happening in a room full of schoolchildren. I started to think about how I wanted to write the story, and I knew I had to set that scene," she adds. "I knew it needed to be a story unfolding like a narrative. I started to break down the chronology of the day, and I thought of that as the road map of this story. . . . I wanted to put readers in the room with the president."

Bush learned of the attacks at an elementary school in Sarasota, Fla. From there he was hustled aboard Air Force One and flown to air bases in Louisiana and Nebraska before returning to the White House that evening to address the nation. "I had to give readers a sense of the movement of the day," Heath says of her story. "There was the sense of him being a captive in Air Force One. The idea that he didn't come back to Washington right away, that in a situation like this he's not in control of his own movements."

Heath's story started to gel not a moment too soon. By the time she saw the crucial pool reports it was already late afternoon, just a few short hours to deadline. She estimates she wrote and reported the story in about 90 minutes. "Basically by the early evening I knew I had enough to work with. I just had to keep my shit together enough to do a story that had to be better than good—and had to be done quickly. A lot of White House reporting is hammering planks together—it's carpentry," Heath says. "Every once in awhile you get a story that's so compelling, you know you're building something really important. You sit up straight and pay more attention. That was true on that day. I felt very emotional about this story. I think it's a lie that reporters have to strip themselves of emotion. This was the most momentous event I'd ever covered, and I didn't want to write a flat story. I had been out on the streets for hours talking to people, and I was really moved. I hope some of that got into the story."

For Heath, the ability to produce compelling news copy on a tight deadline comes from years of experience. A 1989 graduate of Columbia University's journalism school, Heath worked as a reporter at the Anniston (Ala.) Star, the Charlotte Observer and the Raleigh News and Observer before covering the Bush campaign and then landing the White House beat.

She says when she's working on a tight deadline, "I have to have a take on the story. I have to know what I want to say. If you don't have that, nothing you put down on paper matters. Once I have that, I just start writing. My lead may change, but I just get into it and the story takes shape. Sometimes I'll go through my notes with a highlighter and isolate things I know I want to use."

Heath advises aspiring journalists to find an area in which to specialize. "Lose any delusions that it's fine just to be an English major who likes writing. That won't do it for you any more. Decide on an area you want to have some depth in. If you're interested in business, learn about it. If you're interested in politics, really study it. There's less and less opportunity, especially at the big national papers, for people who don't have some real depth and solid, specific expertise."

Here is Heath's account of President Bush's statements and actions in the hours after the Sept. 11, 2001, terrorist attacks:

Washington—President Bush vowed Tuesday night to find and punish the terrorists who attacked the nation and promised not to spare those who might have protected the attackers.

"The search is under way for those who are behind these evil acts," Bush said in a televised address from the Oval Office. "I have directed the full resources of our intelligence and law enforcement communities to find those responsible and to bring them to justice. We will make no distinction between the terrorists who committed these acts and those who harbored them."

Bush named no suspects, nor did he indicate how the United States will respond. Instead, he spoke of victims "in airplanes or in their offices, secretaries, businessmen and women, military and federal workers, moms and dads, friends and neighbors."

He spoke of "quiet, unyielding anger" shared by a nation horrified by television images of crashing airplanes, burning buildings and bloodied hospital stretchers.

"Terrorist attacks can shake the foundations of our biggest buildings, but they cannot touch the foundation of America," he said nearly 12 hours after the first attack on the World Trade Center. "These acts shattered steel, but they cannot dent the steel of American resolve."

Bush implemented national emergency response plans immediately after the first attack on the World Trade Center at 8:45 a.m.

He thanked world leaders who offered help and expressed condolences. Quoting Psalm 23, he pledged that the nation will not be bowed: "Even though I walk through the valley of the shadow of death, I fear no evil, for you are with me."

The Oval Office address was his third of the day on the tragedy, after earlier statements in Florida and Louisiana.

Bush had moved by plane from one secure location to another Tuesday.

Bush learned of the first attack while he was in Sarasota, Fla., to talk about education at an elementary school. He flew from there to secure installations at Air Force bases in Louisiana and Nebraska. He landed at the White House shortly before 7 p.m. Eastern time and proceeded straight to the Oval Office.

"We will find these people, and they will suffer the consequences of taking on this nation," Bush told reporters. "We will do what it takes. No one is going to diminish the spirit of this country."

Vice President Dick Cheney and National Security Adviser Condoleezza Rice had remained at the White House and Defense Secretary Donald Rumsfeld at the Pentagon as Bush made his daylong, circuitous trip.

Bush did not appear preoccupied Tuesday morning as he introduced Education Secretary Rod Paige and shook hands with Sandra Kay Daniels, a teacher at Emma E. Booker Elementary School in Sarasota. The president gave no sign that Rice had just told him by telephone about the first attack on the World Trade Center.

That changed shortly after 9 a.m., when White House Chief of Staff Andy Card entered the room, walked over to the president and whispered the news of the second attack in his ear.

Minutes later, a solemn Bush made his first, brief remarks of the day.

"Terrorism against our nation will not stand," Bush said, calling the attacks "a national tragedy" and asking for a moment of silence.

Bush then headed to Sarasota-Bradenton International Airport, where, in an unusual testament to heightened safety fears, Secret Service agents submitted White House staffers to an extra security check.

Aboard Air Force One, Secret Service agents joined journalists watching live footage of the second World Trade Center tower collapsing and a news report of the attack on the Pentagon, in Arlington, Va.

Air Force One, accompanied by a military escort that included fighter jets, headed west at 40,000 feet after a protracted takeoff. Flying with Bush were Card, senior political adviser Karl Rove, communications director Dan Bartlett, education adviser Sandy Kress, press secretary Ari Fleischer and U.S. Rep. Dan Miller (R-Fla.).

Bush visited a number of military sites Tuesday, heading first to Barksdale Air Force Base, La., and then to Orfutt Air Force Base, Neb., where he visited the deep underground bunkers of the U.S. Strategic Command.

Former Secretary of State Alexander Haig told CNN the relocation sites are "armed with communication, living facilities."

At Barksdale, Miller, Kress, a handful of Secret Service agents, a White House staffer and print reporters were removed from the plane. Bush, his top aides and the rest traveled on to Nebraska.

Fleischer later told reporters Bush spoke repeatedly with Cheney while at Barksdale.

At Barksdale, Bush said military installations worldwide had been placed on highest alert, and he pledged to retaliate.

"Make no mistake, the United States will hunt down and punish those responsible for these cowardly acts," Bush said. ". . . We have been in touch with the leaders of Congress and with world leaders to assure them that we will do whatever is necessary to protect America and Americans."

Citing security precautions, administration officials did not release information on the president's schedule until after Bush landed at the secure military installations.

About 3:30 p.m., Bush, after landing in Nebraska, reportedly convened a late-afternoon teleconference of the National Security Council. Not long afterward, Karen Hughes, counselor to the president, spoke to the nation from FBI headquarters in Washington.

Hughes said the Secret Service had "immediately" secured Bush, Cheney and House Speaker Dennis Hastert (R-Ill.) and that U.S. embassies and military forces worldwide were put on alert.

"President Bush has committed the full resource of our intelligence and law-enforcement communities to identify and bring to swift justice those responsible for these despicable attacks," Hughes said. "Our fellow citizens and our freedom came under attack today, and no one should doubt America's resolve."

Rumsfeld later told reporters. "The Pentagon's functioning. It'll be in business tomorrow."

At the White House on Tuesday morning, White House staffers were glued to television news reports of the World Trade Center attacks. About 9:30 a.m., Commerce Department worker Greg Jenkins, who has been on loan to the White House, heard a standard fire alarm announcement over the intercom at the Old Executive Office Building. But staffers knew enough to realize what was happening, Jenkins said.

About 100 reporters and a handful of White House staffers gathered on a corner that became a makeshift press center across from the White House. There, a junior White House spokeswoman became the only source of information, and she could not get a cell phone connection, either. "If I tell you guys to run, run fast," she said, remembering a Secret Service agent who evacuated her. "We thought he was joking, at first."

© 2002, Cox News Service. Reprinted with permission.

INTERNET EXERCISES

A wide variety of speeches—from historically important talks delivered decades ago to ones given just hours ago—are available on the Web and can be used as the basis for newswriting exercises.

The White House—**http://www.whitehouse.gov**—makes available recent addresses by the president as well as the transcripts of press briefings.

Historical speeches—both in print and streaming audio formats—are available from The History Channel—**http://www.historychannel.com**—and at PBS' Great American Speeches site—**http://www.pbs.org/greatspeeches/**.

Sweet Briar College has an excellent collection of speeches given by women at **http://gos.sbc.edu/**.

George Washington University's Speech and Transcript Center is an excellent archive of recent political speeches and press conferences—**http://gwis2.circ.gwu.edu/~gprice/speech.htm**.

Pentagon speeches and press conferences can be found at **http://www.defenselink.mil/speeches/**.

Speeches and press conferences given by the mayor of New York City can be found at **http://www.nyc.gov/html/om/html/speeches.html**.

Press conferences held by Chinese government officials can be found at **http://www.china.org.cn/e-news/**.

BEYOND THE CLASSROOM

Public speeches and seminars are held frequently on most college campuses. Check your school's event listings for such a speech and cover it. Write it up for the student newspaper. Or check your local paper for listings of such events and attend one in your community. Groups like the Rotary Club have monthly meetings in which they often invite guest speakers.

chapter eight

Meetings

Covering the cops may be more exciting. Following a big court case may be more glamorous. But no beat is as important to your readers as coverage of the local government and school board—and this means covering meetings.

Reporters may complain that writing about meetings can be dull. Sometimes that's true. But just as often, town government and school board meetings can be raucous, unruly gatherings of dozens or even hundreds of community residents. That's because issues of real importance to your community are debated there, and passions can run high. And while the activities of the state and federal government can seem very distant, actions taken by town governments and school boards directly affect your readers' lives—and readers know it.

When the local town council decides, for instance, to install parking meters on downtown streets after years of free parking, that's an action your readers will notice. Likewise, if your local school board is debating whether to ban certain books from the school libraries, chances are that's an issue your readers will feel strongly about, no matter which side they take. And if they feel strongly enough about an issue, they'll show up at a town government or school board meeting to let their opinion be heard—sometimes loudly.

Local government, whether in the form of a city council, county commission or village board, oversees a wide range of services in the community—from street cleaning and parks maintenance to garbage collection and the operation of the local library. Typically, local government consists of a mayor and a town council, all of whom are elected officials. These officials enact laws that dictate how all sorts of activities can be performed. For example, if you want to build a house or start a business, chances are you'll need a permit from your local government.

Likewise, local school boards, which also generally consist of elected officials, have broad responsibility for virtually every aspect of how the schools are run—from what and how children are taught to the maintenance of the buildings they use and how much their teachers are paid. To provide all these services, local governments and school boards need money. To get money, of course, they must levy taxes.

That brings us to the other important reason why readers closely follow the activities of their town and schools. Readers as a rule are almost always very concerned with any action that affects how much they pay in taxes. As we noted earlier, readers feel they have more say in local issues. While many people might not like how much they must pay in state or federal taxes, most feel there's little they can do about it. But taxes enacted on the local level are another matter.

Local governments and school boards can levy a variety of different kinds of taxes—sales, income, and so on—but their biggest source of revenue is something called the property tax. This tax is based on the value of one's home. So people with more expensive homes pay more in property taxes. The technical term for the tax is mill levy. Each mill is worth one-tenth of 1 cent. The amount of property tax one pays is calculated by multiplying the mill amount by every $100 of the value of one's home. Typically, town governments and school boards develop a budget for the coming year. The budget outlines how much money they will need to raise in property taxes in order to meet their operating expenses.

Let's say the Centerville City Council's budget mandates that $10 million must be raised in property taxes. The property tax, or mill levy, will be the amount of taxes needed to be collected divided by the value of all homes in Centerville. If the value of all homes in Centerville is $100 million, the formula would look like this:

Mill levy = $10 million ÷ $100 million, or 10 ÷ 100, or 0.1

Mill levy = 1 cent on each $1 of the value of property, or $1 for each $100 of valuation, or $10 for each $1,000 of valuation

Let's say the assessed value of the average home in Centerville is $50,000. It's then just a matter of simple multiplication to figure out what that homeowner would pay in property taxes: 50 × $10 = $500. Likewise, the owner of a home whose assessed value is $100,000 would pay $1,000.

Property taxes are calculated using the assessed value of one's home, which is much different—and generally much lower—than the actual market value. Local governments assess the value of residential properties.

WRITING THE STORY

Chapter 7 discusses the danger of covering speeches in chronological order. If the most important thing a speaker says comes in the last five minutes of his talk, that has to come at the beginning of your story, not the end. The same is true of town government and school board meetings. Town governments and school boards deal with a wide range of issues, some important and interesting, some mundane and dull. The reporter covering these meetings must quickly learn to separate the wheat from the chaff.

Let's say you're covering a Centerville City Council meeting. At the start of the meeting the council agrees to purchase more paper clips for the town secretary. At the end of the meeting councilors vote to raise property taxes 5 percent. Which issue should come first in your story? Using the guidelines outlined in Chapter 1 for deciding what is newsworthy, it's pretty easy to see that the tax hike is bigger news. It affects far more of your readers, and in a fairly significant way. Chances are, the only person interested in the paper clips vote is the secretary. Reporters covering government meetings focus on the most newsworthy issues being debated. Less important items are put at the bottom of the story or left out altogether. Editors generally want meetings stories to focus leads on one issue. Avoid leads that try to cram too many issues into the top of the story or that are too general. For example:

The Centerville City Council met last night to discuss property taxes, parks maintenance and upcoming elections for mayor.

The Centerville City Council last night took up the issue of property taxes.

The first lead reads like a laundry list, and the second lead tells the reader nothing, other than the fact that the meeting was last night and property taxes were discussed. Readers want leads that give them hard information quickly. Find the most important issue discussed, and make that your lead. Also, focus on specific actions taken at the meeting. As the old saying goes, actions speak louder than words. And concrete actions generally make for good leads. Example:

The Centerville City Council last night raised property taxes 3 percent.

BE PREPARED

Walk into a town council or school board meeting cold, and you're bound to be dazed and confused within minutes. Councilors and school board members will be discussing complex issues you know nothing about, and you'll be struggling to keep up by scribbling notes. But all the note-taking won't help if you don't understand what's going on. And you certainly won't be able to write a clear, lucid story if you don't have a clue about the issues being discussed.

When covering a meeting, it's a good idea to get a copy of the agenda ahead of time (these can usually be obtained from town hall or the school board office) to give you a head start on deciding what's important and what's not. It also gives you an opportunity to research issues you're not up on. Don't be afraid to call school board or town officials before a meeting to make sure you understand what's going to be discussed. And make sure to do plenty of interviews after the meeting has ended—again, to aid your own understanding of the discussion.

Make sure you get the correct spelling of everyone's names. And jot down phone numbers for everyone you interview. Reporters sitting down to write a story often find they have a few more questions that need answering or facts that need checking. Having phone numbers handy makes such checks much easier.

QUICK TIPS

- Don't cover meetings in chronological order. Put important items at the top of your story, less important items at the bottom.
- Focus on one issue in the lead.
- Focus your lead on any concrete actions taken by the town council or school board. Actions speak louder than words.
- Look for issues and actions that affect people. The more people affected by something the town council or school board does, the bigger the story.

exercise one

Write a story based on the following information. Deadline: 30 minutes.

You're covering a meeting of the Langhorne Manor Town Council. Langhorne Manor is a tiny, half-square-mile borough with a population of about 800. The town has a seven-member, part-time police force.

Last year the town's police chief, Robert Dansbury, left the job for medical reasons. He formally resigned several months ago. Since Dansbury's departure, Sgt. Russell Bumm has been acting chief. At today's meeting the board officially appointed Bumm the new police chief.

Here's some background information on Bumm: He's 38 years old, married with two children, lives in nearby Levittown. He grew up in Langhorne Borough and attended Neshaminy High School and Temple University's police academy. He's been an officer in the Langhorne Manor Police Department since 1992 and a full-time officer with the Upper Southampton Police Department since 1988. He also worked in the Penndel Police Department, the Bucks County police radio room and the Bucks County Courthouse. "Russell has a lot of street experience and he knows the direction we want to go in," Langhorne Manor mayor Gerry Seader tells you.

As one of his first tasks, Bumm said he'd like to update the department's policies and procedures. "This is a nice, quiet town. We don't have any businesses. We really don't have much trouble here," said Bumm.

exercise two

Write a story based on the following information. Deadline: 40 minutes.

You're covering the Marshfield School Board, which oversees the public schools in Marshfield, a suburb of Centerville. Here are your notes from tonight's meeting:

- Board begins meeting by awarding the district's Teacher of the Year honor to Evelyn Hansen, a math teacher at Dawson High School. Hansen "has made subjects like trigonometry and calculus interesting, understandable and even exciting to students for more than 25 years," says board President Irving Kroning as he hands Hansen a plaque. The award is based on polling of teachers and students districtwide.
- Board hears a report from Jason Freedman, principal of the Allgren Middle School. He says construction on the new addition to the

school is going well and should be completed by the target date of next July, in time for the fall semester. The addition consists of a computer lab and two classrooms. The project has been budgeted at $850,000; Freedman says he doesn't expect any cost overruns.

- Board hears public testimony from the group Parents for the Christian Way, which wants to ban more than a dozen books from the district's high school libraries, including "Catcher in the Rye," "The Color Purple" and "Our Bodies, Ourselves." The group presents the board with a petition bearing 5,000 signatures asking that the books be banned. "These books are filled with filth, depravity and godlessness," group President Grace Shanker tells the board. "They have no place in our children's schools, even the high schools." Shanker's comments get scattered applause and some boos from the audience of about 100 people. In a public comment session that follows, more than a dozen people speak, some in support of the measure, others opposed. Sarah Vopat, an English teacher at Centerville State College, tells the board, "Many of these books are examples of classic American literature. Banning them would be a disgrace. This religious group might have you believe otherwise, but censorship is not the American way." Vopat, like Shanker, gets a mix of applause and boos. The board, after hearing public comment for more than an hour, votes to take the matter under advisement.

When you get back to the newsroom, the city editor tells you to get some background information from the Internet about other attempts around the country to ban books in schools.

exercise three

Write a story based on the following information. Deadline: 45 minutes.

You're covering the Centerville City Council. Here are your notes from the meeting:

- Council hears a report from Centerville zoning board. The board has recommended that the council approve a request from BB Inc., to build a new Burger Boy restaurant at a vacant lot at the corner of 16th and Main Streets. Council members approve the request unanimously.
- Council approves a request from the city's Parks and Recreation Department to build a large utility garage near the department's offices. Parks and Recreation Commissioner Joe Fazolla tells the council the shed, which will be used to house the city's lawn mowers, should cost about $10,000 to build.
- Council hears testimony about a measure to raise the city income tax from 1 percent to 2 percent. Mayor John Smith, who proposed the hike several months ago, tells the board the city is facing a $12 million budget deficit this year, and an income tax increase for Centerville residents is the only way to make up the shortfall. "We have to plug this budget gap," he tells the council. Councilwoman Jane Tornada is the most outspoken opponent of the measure. "The taxpayers of Centerville should not have to bear this burden. Mayor Smith's tax-and-spend administration should be slashing the city budget, not raising taxes." But Smith responds that the city budget has already been cut to the bone. After much debate, the council passes the tax hike by a 6-4 vote. About 300 members of the public are attending the meeting, and most boo loudly. After the meeting you interview Centerville resident Bob Franklin, who works at a shoe store on Main Street. "This tax increase is ridiculous," he tells you. "The city keeps spending more and more and it's the little people like me who have to foot the bill." You also interview Jane Bryson, who works at an art gallery in Centerville. "No one wants to pay more taxes, but if this is what it takes to keep the city running, then we don't have much choice." As you're leaving the meeting, you check with city budget director Pete Tillson, who tells you that the income of the average Centerville resident is $45,000.

Write a story based on the following information. Deadline: one hour.

You're covering a meeting of the Neshaminy School Board. The board has unanimously passed a preliminary budget for the coming year. The total amount of the budget is $123,239,238, down from the $130 million originally proposed. Joseph Paradise, the district's business manager, tells you the budget was trimmed in several ways:

- By working with insurance companies, the board cut employee health insurance by $325,000.
- The state has reduced the district's contribution to the state pension fund by $1.6 million.
- Another $564,000 will be saved in salaries because 35 teachers have retired, and the salaries of new teachers replacing them will be lower.

- Two full-time academic enrichment positions have been eliminated.

Paradise says the budget is still a work in progress and the board is continuing to make cuts. The final budget will be voted on next month. "We're working on further cuts in technology, overall maintenance, supplies, travel reductions, vehicle replacements and several others," he says.

The original budget would have meant a 59.9-mill increase, roughly a $400 yearly increase for the average taxpayer in the district. The new budget has a 34.4-mill increase. The average home in the district is assessed at $6,600. Calculate what the average taxpayer would pay under the new budget, and include that in your story (see Appendix B).

Write a story based on the following information. Deadline: one hour.

You're covering the Northampton Board of Supervisors. Here are your notes:

Township manager Bruce Townsend says next year's budget will be bigger for three reasons. First, medical costs are rising. Two years ago medical costs totaled about $572,000. Next year, those are expected to run $916,000. Second, lower interest rates mean the township is making less money on its investments. Previously, the township could count on making $200,000 or more annually on its investments. Now, "our investment [returns] have been cut in half," he says. Third, fire vehicles and equipment need to be replaced. Townsend says the yearly appropriation for buying new fire equipment will be increased by about $31,000 to a total of $154,000. "For the past few years, fire equipment has been costing more money," Townsend says.

The Board is proposing a $36 million budget for next year. That represents a 2.75-mill increase to 15.65 mills, or a 21 percent hike in the property tax. That means a Northampton resident whose home is assessed at $10,650—the township average—would pay a total of $165.90 in real estate taxes next year, a $28.60 increase over this year. Townsend says one-half mill of the increase would be devoted to buying new fire equipment.

Townsend also says the annual fee for trash collection will increase by $30 next year, to $215. He says the increase is necessary to wipe out the deficit for trash collection that the township had been running in recent years.

The budget is on display at the municipal building until Dec. 12, when the supervisors are due to vote for final adoption.

exercise six

Write a story based on the following information. Deadline: one hour.

You're covering a meeting of the Neshaminy School Board. Several parents of Neshaminy Middle School students have come to the meeting because they are upset that their children are being shown Channel One, a news-oriented network shown at various schools around the country. Last year, Neshaminy started airing the show at Poquessing Middle School in Feasterville. It was successful enough that the board expanded it this year to its three other middle schools. The programs began airing earlier this month in the middle schools. In exchange for airing daily news-oriented segments, Channel One promoters lend the district equipment, including color TV sets, a fixed satellite dish and VCRs for the schools. It also provides schoolwide cable wiring. But Margie and Philip Gillies of Langhorne tell the board that during homeroom recently, their sixth-grade daughter has been shown video clips of rocker Marilyn Manson and scenes of Afghan fighters pointing guns into a TV camera lens. The couple says they don't let their daughter watch TV programs containing graphic violence and guns at home. "Images of war are not appropriate for children," Philip Gillies tells the board. "This is se-

rious. This has long-lasting [effects on] children." The couple says programs dealing with terrorism in America and the war in Afghanistan are too mature for middle-school-age children. Margie Gillies said she decided to speak to the board after seeing a program shown to Neshaminy Middle School students last week in which the word "anthrax" was used seven times in the first 90 seconds. Another segment was billed as "when tough economic times take a toll on the family." "This is what our kids are viewing," she says. The couple also note that at Neshaminy High School, the faculty apparently has rejected a proposal to bring Channel One programming to the school.

Dave Fleshier, another parent of a sixth-grader, also tells the board he's concerned about Channel One's program content. He suggests the board reconsider its relationship with the company. School Board President Ed Stack, with the consensus of the board, agrees to place Channel One as a topic for discussion and review at the board's education development committee next month.

Get some background on Channel One from the Internet, then write your story.

Real REPORTER: **Ross Markman**

As one of just three reporters on the tiny Havre Daily News (circulation 4,500) in north central Montana, Ross Markman covers county government, city government and the local schools—any one of which might be an entirely separate beat at a larger newspaper. But Markman says being on a small paper gives him lots of great experience because he sometimes writes 10 or more articles a week—often on a tight deadline. So while Markman has only been in the news business a few years, he's already a real pro at banging out news copy quickly; for example, when he covers meetings of the Havre City Council on Monday nights, he usually finishes his story within an hour after the meeting has ended.

The topic at one recent meeting was one that town governments everywhere deal with—parking. People were exceeding the two-hour parking limit on downtown streets, creating a parking crunch. "The mayor wanted to get cars off the street that don't belong there," Markman recalls, because "some downtown business owners had complained."

Markman covered the meeting and wrote the story in about 30 minutes. To write that quickly, he says, a reporter has to do his homework *before* the meeting ever starts. "I knew about the issue beforehand from talking to people. The mayor had been telling me what was going on. It's key, if you're writing on deadline, to get background material ahead of time on the issues being discussed."

Reporters should always find out the agenda of a city council or school board meeting before long before it begins, Markman says. That's easy enough to do by contacting city or school officials. And if an important issue is going to be discussed, do some research on it so you understand what's going on when the meeting begins, Markman says. It makes it easier to write the story quickly.

Markman sometimes writes background copy—what reporters sometimes call B-copy—before the meeting starts. That way, when the meeting is over, he can simply "top" the background copy with whatever new information comes out of the meeting. He says there's no excuse for a reporter not doing this kind of preparation. "You can never say, 'I don't know anything about an issue,'" he says. "When you come into a newspaper you can't use that excuse. You have to find out."

Another key to covering meetings is figuring out how to begin the story. If several different issues are being discussed, how does Markman decide what the lead of his story will be? "You have to determine what's newsworthy," he says. "I think of issues in terms of how they affect people. Even a little ordinance the city council is passing may affect a lot of people. Everything they do in these meetings has an effect on somebody." The more people affected by an issue, the bigger the story.

Boring stuff of interest to only a tiny number of people—such as the city council agreeing to buy more paper clips for the mayor's secretary—can be put at the bottom of a story or left out altogether. But Markman says if several important issues are taken up at one meeting, he may write a separate story for each issue.

Markman, a Pennsylvania native, earned his associate's degree in liberal arts at Bucks County Community College, taking just one journalism class. While still a student, he landed a part-time clerical job at the Bucks County Courier Times, which led to a two-year reporting internship. Newspaper internships, which can last anywhere from 12 weeks over the summer to several years, give college students the chance to get real-life experience at a professional newspaper. Markman covered local government in Newtown, a small suburban community about 40 miles north of Philadelphia. He found the experience invaluable.

"When I started I knew nothing," he recalls. "An editor took me under her wing and I ended up learning a lot. When the internship ended, Markman headed west and landed a reporting job in Havre. He plans to return to college and complete his bachelor's degree after getting a few years of reporting experience under his belt. "I may go back and finish my degree," Markman says. "But I think real work experience is more important. I've learned so much on the job."

Markman's experience highlights another exciting aspect of the life of a reporter—the ability to work in any part of the country—or, indeed, the world. "Coming out to Montana from the East Coast was really scary," Markman says. "But it was something I felt I had to do. I wanted to see what it was like to live and work somewhere else."

Here is Ross Markman's city council story:

The Havre City Council Monday night decided to give the Havre business community a chance to determine its own fate—and that of parking in the city's main shopping area.

Two weeks ago, Havre Mayor Bob Rice called for something to be done about the parking crunch in the business district, which, according to city ordinance, is bounded by First Street on the north, Fourth Street on the south, First Avenue on the west and Fifth Avenue on the east.

Rice said he receives several phone calls a week from area shopkeepers claiming that people are exceeding the two-hour parking limit the ordinance established.

None of those business owners showed up Monday night, Rice noted.

"The three people that hollered the most, the three people who called me the most are not even here," he said.

Murray Barkus, owner of Barkus Home Center on Second Street, said two weeks ago that vehicles are routinely parked outside his store for several hours, sometimes days at a time. The problem, he said, is a combination of employees of other businesses, movie theater patrons and Second Street apartment renters—all parking in front of his and other stores.

Barkus said he's tried asking people to move their vehicles during the day, but has been unsuccessful.

Barkus did not attend Monday night's meeting.

In fact, only two storeowners were in attendance—Larry DeRosa of Northern Electronics and Janine Donoven of JM Donoven Design in Fine Jewelry.

"We're not after the people who are downtown shopping," said DeRosa, whose business is on First Street. "We need to do something about the guy who parks there all day long."

Writing tickets, he said, is not the answer.

"This is not necessarily an issue that needs to be policed. I don't think that's what we're after," DeRosa said.

Donoven agreed.

"I don't want to have to sign my name on the dotted line of a ticket. That person will never shop at my store again," she said. "I think the business community really needs to take it upon themselves to talk to their employees."

Debbie Vandeberg, executive director of the Havre Area Chamber of Commerce, proposed mailing a survey to stores in the business district. The survey would ask owners what they suggest should be done to quell the parking problem.

"It's an option. It's up at the discretion of the business community," Vandeberg said today of the survey.

"We've gotten lazy. We've allowed our employees to get lazy," she added. "I think an educational process needs to be done. If there's an ordinance, you either need to sign and enforce it—or get rid of it."

Havre is no stranger to two-hour parking signs. About eight years ago, the signs were removed under an agreement between the city and the Chamber, city Public Works Director Dave Peterson said.

The ordinance, however, remained on the books.

"We do have an ordinance in effect. If we're going to enforce it, then the signs have to go back up," Council President Rick Pierson said. "Our hands aren't tied. We can enforce this ordinance."

Rice said he did an informal survey of businesses Monday and found that 75 percent don't want the city to put the signs back up, and half don't think parking is a problem.

Enforcing a two-hour limit is a challenge, Havre Assistant Police Chief Mark Stolen said.

"To enforce it, not only do you need the signs up, you need some way to prove that a vehicle was there that long," Stolen said.

That could mean marking tires with chalk, something council member Allen "Woody" Woodwick said is impractical.

"How will they know who is shopping and who has just been parked there?" he said. "Do you want to reward somebody who actually stopped for two hours to shop downtown with a ticket?"

Reprinted with permission from the Havre Daily News.

INTERNET EXERCISES

- Journalism Professor Rich Cameron has created a terrific online city council news-writing exercise. It can be found at **http://www.rcameron.com/journalism/citycouncil/index.html**.

- Many cities and towns publish the minutes or transcripts from their government meetings online. These can be used as the basis for a news story. See if you can find the Web site for your city or town and see if such transcripts are online. Or you can find minutes from city councils around the country by checking State and Local Government on the Net, which has links to cities and towns nationwide. The url is: **http://www.statelocalgov.net**.

- You can also do a Google search for "City Council meeting minutes," or check specific cities and towns. Here are some examples:

  City of Cedar Rapids: **http://www.cedar-rapids.org/council/meetings.asp**

  City of Austin: **http://www.ci.austin.tx.us/council/**

  City of Boston: **http://www.cityofboston.com/citycouncil/default.asp**

  City of Eugene: **http://www.ci.eugene.or.us/Council/minutes.htm**

  City of Arlington: **http://www.ci.arlington.tx.us/citycouncil/minutes.html**

- Many cities and towns also publish their annual budgets online. These too can be used as the basis for newswriting exercises. Again, do a Google search for city budgets. Here are just a few examples:

  Town of Orange, Va., budget: **http://www.townoforangeva.org/government/budget.htm**

  Town of West Hartford budget: **http://www.west-hartford.com/Government/Budget/welcomepage.htm**

  Town of Harvard, Mass., budget: **http://www.harvard.ma.us/townbudget.htm**

  City of Fort Wayne budget: **http://cityoffortwayne.org/budget/**

  City of Indianapolis budget: **http://www.indygov.org/controller/**

BEYOND THE CLASSROOM

1. Find the time and location of a town government or school board meeting near you and go cover it. Meeting times are often listed in local newspapers and on those papers' Web sites. Or you can check the Web site of your local city or town. Try to get a copy of the meeting's agenda before you go. If you have questions about what's being discussed, call some town council or school board members and ask them to explain it to you.

2. Get a copy of this year's budget from your local town council or school board. Go over the numbers carefully, then use them to write a story in which you outline the most important aspects of the budget for your readers. Write the story as if you were writing it for your local paper.

9

Sports

*f*rom Red Smith to Frank Deford and Bill Lyon, some of the best writing in journalism has come from the sports section. Sports journalism often moves far beyond the boundaries of the five W's and the H, and instead turns toward a more creative, storytelling kind of approach. It's a style similar to feature writing (this book explores feature writing methods in Chapter 13. If you're an aspiring sportswriter, you can study that chapter and use its techniques as you begin to cover sports). But this chapter will focus on the basics of straight sports writing, which in many ways is much like straight newswriting.

There are two key elements that should go into the lead of any straight sports story. The first is the score. This seems obvious, but it's surprising how many beginning sportswriters forget to put a game's final score at the top of the story.

The second key lead element is the high point, or highlight, of the game. It's the moment—or moments—that make the basketball game or hockey match or skating competition you're covering stand out from all the others. One example of this would be when a player scores a game-winning goal or point with just seconds left on the clock. Or maybe one player carries the team on his back, scoring a huge number of points (think Michael Jordan or Allen Iverson). Or maybe it's the previously unheralded player who steps up to the plate and sends the ball out of the park.

Whatever makes the game dramatic and exciting is what you want to put into your lead. Frequently this means focusing on an individual. While the most popular sports in this country are generally team endeavors (football, basketball, baseball), it's the role of the individual player that often makes the game interesting. Sports stories, after all, are people stories, and it's the triumphs and travails of individual athletes that make sports so fascinating—and make the sports section one of the most widely read in the paper.

Here's an example of a straight sports lead:

> *Eddie Jackson scored 26 points and slam-dunked the game-winning shot with two seconds left to lead Pennsfield High School to a 78-76 upset victory over basketball powerhouse Parkland High last night.*

Notice the dramatic elements in the lead: the individual effort of high-scorer Eddie Jackson, his last-second slam-dunk, the fact that this is an upset victory over a better team. And, of course, there's the score.

The rest of the story should elaborate on the lead and paint a complete picture of the game. A good sports story should describe momentum-changing plays and scores, highlight standout players on both teams, wrap in post-game quotes from players and coaches, and examine the significance of the game in the league standings.

exercise one

Write a story based on the following information. Deadline: 30 minutes.

You're covering a boys' basketball game between Conwell-Egan High School (the Eagles) and Bensalem High (the Owls). Here are your notes from the game:

Andrew Holland scored a game-high 22 points for Conwell-Egan. Ryan McMullin led the Bensalem Owls with 18 points and 10 rebounds. The Owls' Brandon Davis added 16 points, including four three-pointers, and grabbed 10 rebounds. Joe Rogers had 10 rebounds for Bensalem. The Owls also had 18 turnovers and struggled at the foul line, going 15 for 26. Conwell-Egan Assistant coach Larry Breiner tells you it's been this way all season. He says, "We've been winning ugly. We're happy to be 4-0, but we still have a lot of work to do." Bensalem is 0-3. Final score: Bensalem 54, Conwell-Egan 46.

exercise two

Write a story based on the following information. Deadline: 30 minutes.

You're covering a girls' basketball game between John F. Kennedy High School (the Tigers) and Pennsfield Academy High (the Falcons). Here are your notes from the game:

For Kennedy, Nancy Corn scored a game-high 21 points, including two three-point goals; Niki Jackson scored 14 points; Millie Horsham added 12 points and made 10 rebounds. For Pennsfield, Terri Levonne scored 18 points; Lucy Wong scored 10 points and made 8 rebounds.

Kennedy is 3-2, Pennsfield is 1-4. Kennedy won just three games last season. In just three weeks this season, the team has already equaled that total. First-year coach Frank Robelot tells you, "We played really well as a team today. The girls are really playing well together." Final score: Kennedy 58, Pennsfield 40.

exercise three

Write a story based on the following information. Deadline: 30 minutes.

You're covering the championship game of the Babe Ruth baseball tournament for 14-year-olds. The two teams are Levittown and Tri-Township. Here are your notes from the game:

Levittown takes a 1-0 lead in the first inning. Mike Rugghia walks and scores on a triple by Brian Herman. Tri-Township ties the score in the third inning. Score remains 1-1 until the top of the seventh, when Levittown scores four runs: John Lalli hits a two-run double, John Malloy hits an RBI single, and pinch-hitter Paul Sheerbaum doubles in another run. Rugghia pitches the first five innings for Levittown. Herman pitches the final two. Levittown now advances to the state tournament, which begins July 19 at Tri-Township. Levittown will open the tournament against Tri-Township. Levittown won the tournament despite dropping a 2-1 decision to Middletown in the first round. After that, Levittown beat Newtown (11-1), Middletown (4-3) and Lower Southampton (6-0) before sweeping Tri-Township. Tri-Township went 2-2 in the tournament. The team had a first-round bye, then beat Middletown and Lower Southampton to advance to the final. Levittown coach Frank Dea says, "It was a tough tournament. There were some good teams. That Tri-Township team is a tough, tough ball club." Of the tournament overall, he says, "It was an uphill battle, that's for sure. Our pitching and defense really carried us through the tournament." Dea says he expects a good game against Tri-Township in the state tournament. "They don't want us, and we don't want them," he said.

exercise four

Write a story based on the following information. Deadline: 40 minutes.

You're covering a boys' basketball game between Pennsbury High School and Council Rock High. Here are your notes from the game:

Brian Romig led Pennsbury (13-11) with 17 points; Ben Luber led Council Rock (9-14) with 24. Council Rock led throughout the second half, but missed several key free throws down the stretch. Pennsbury forced the game into overtime as Justin Johnson tipped in a missed shot with two seconds remaining in regulation. Freshman Jason Vegotsky scored five of his 10 points in overtime; he also hit the game-winning shot with three seconds remaining in overtime. Vegotsky got the ball, forced his defender to the right, pulled up and drilled the game-winner from about 10 feet out. Pennsbury coach Frank Sciolla tells you he had no doubt about having

Vegotsky take the final shot. "There wasn't much of a question it was going to him," Sciolla says. "He's played more than any freshman has played here. He's probably hit that shot in his driveway at home a couple thousand times. It's his shot. I don't treat him like a freshman, and he doesn't play like one." After the game Vegotsky tells you, "It was pretty crazy. Both teams played unreal. I don't know what a playoff atmosphere is like, but this is the most amazing thing I've ever seen." He adds, "I've always had confidence. But it seems like I get more and more confidence each time we play or practice. I just made my move, and took the shot. It feels great." Council Rock coach Buff Radick tells you, "I'm an old school basketball player and coach, and one of the most important parts of the game is shooting free throws. We had three one-and-ones with a four-point lead and missed them all. The game should have been over. It was a good high school basketball game, and you have to give (Pennsbury) credit, but we have to realize that free throws are an important part of the game. Tonight, it cost us a basketball game." Final score: Pennsbury 53, Council Rock 51.

exercise five

Write a story based on the following information. Deadline: 45 minutes.

You're covering a high school football game between the George School and visiting Perkiomen High. Here are your notes from the game:

George School took an early 7-0 lead on a Rob Waters run. Perkiomen came back with a touchdown in each of the first three quarters, including a two-point conversion in the second quarter on an option play caught by Sean Singletary, nephew of former Chicago Bears great Mike Singletary. Larry Andrews' 81-yard TD run gave Perkiomen School a 22-7 lead in the third quarter. George School bounced back in the fourth, when Waters rushed for another touchdown. He ended the day with 184 yards rushing. But Perkiomen sealed the win with a safety in the fourth period. After the game, George School quarterback Jon Compitello says, "I wish we could have won, but what it all comes down to is the experience. It's about having fun and the brothership." George School coach John Gleeson says, "These kids played their hearts out. They gave everything they could, especially the seniors." George School ends the year 4-4, losing its last three games after winning four in a row at one point. The game is the last one to be played together by George School senior split ends Ben Fisher and Ryan Mellon. The two Doylestown residents have been best friends since first grade. They have been attending school together ever since they can remember. But they'll be going to different colleges next fall. "It's real tough," Mellon says after the game. "It's bittersweet. You always want to win your last game, but we battled the whole way. That's the way to go out. It still hasn't sunk it yet that my high school football career is over." Fisher adds, "The four years I put into this program, all the pain, the sweat, the blood, I wouldn't trade it for anything. I look at these 30 guys as my second family. It really hurts to lose the last one. It's been great for the team to have the two split ends as best friends, but next year, we'll be going to different schools, so that'll be different." Final score: Perkiomen 24, George School 14.

Real REPORTER: **Robb Luehr**

For sportswriters, producing copy on an extremely tight deadline is a way of life. In many sports, night games are commonplace, which means reporters covering them often have just a matter of hours or even minutes to write a story after the last touchdown, goal or run has been scored.

Robb Luehr, a sportswriter for the Journal Times in Racine, Wis., faced just such a challenge covering a high school girls' soccer match. The match began at 7 p.m. and ended about two hours later. By the time he'd gotten back to the Journal Times newsroom it was just over an hour before deadline. Luehr did what reporters often do in such situations—he put together much of the article in his head during the drive back to the newsroom. So by the time he sat down at a computer to write, he had much of the story's structure—its skeleton—in place.

In fact, Luehr says he starts to think of the lead of his stories even before the game ends. He does this by looking for elements that stand out and make the game exciting. For example, one player may have an especially good game and outshine her teammates. Or there might be a big momentum shift between two teams in a seesaw battle for points. It could be an upset victory, a David vs. Goliath struggle. Or it may be a case of a much stronger team simply whipping the other side. Whatever the case, finding the lead means watching the game for trends like these, Luehr says.

"There's no set way to do it," he says. "Sometimes it's the unsung hero. I like that angle. A guy might do nothing during the whole game, then suddenly take over the game and carry the team on his back. You formulate your lead as things happen. Sometimes doing the lead is the hardest part. But if you get that done, you can move on to the rest of the story."

In the girls' soccer match, the defending Division 1 state champions, Milwaukee Pius XI, were ahead 2-0 with just over 30 minutes left in regulation. The upstart Horlick High School team from Racine appeared soundly beaten. But then the momentum shifted. Horlick sophomore Michelle Lizotte scored two goals—the second came with just 31 seconds left in regulation—and a teammate added another to lead Horlick to a 3-2 victory. It was a classic upset. But Luehr noticed another element that he found interesting—in the second half, the Horlick team had the wind at its back. "Their style of play is long kicks from the back to the front of the field, so the tailwind played right into their hands," Luehr says.

Luehr managed to work all of these elements—the underdog beating the champion, the last-minute victory goal, the tailwind—into his story. But to get them into his article, Luehr had to first observe them and jot them down in his notebook. A casual sports fan doesn't have to worry about such things. But sportswriters need to observe a game they way a scientist examines a slide under a microscope—carefully and methodically. "You need to follow the action closely," Luehr says. "Chart when shots are taken, watch for when a team has a chance to score, and keep a running tab of who scores."

Without solid, thorough reporting, you can't produce well-written sports stories, Luehr says. For example, he makes sure to interview both the coaches and some of the players after games. When possible, he gets a printout of the game's stats (such data are often provided to reporters after games), which is necessary if the writer needs to prepare an agate box to go along with his story.

Luehr also tapes all his post-game interviews. When he sits down to write, he listens to his tape recorder and types the contents of the interviews into the computer, so the quotes are on his computer screen and can be easily plugged into his story.

Luehr says it's also important to make a distinction between covering big-league sports, which is generally done only by the most experienced sportswriters, and writing about high school and college teams, which is what the vast majority of sportswriters on local papers cover. Sportswriters covering the big leagues tend to be very critical of players and teams that don't win. After all, many players in the NFL, NBA and major league baseball are earning millions of dollars. They are held to a very high standard, and rightly so.

But at the college, and especially the high school levels, sportswriters generally exercise more sensitivity. After all, the athletes are not being paid. They're playing sports at the amateur level for the love of the game; few will ever become rich or famous for playing a sport. So sportswriters generally don't subject scholastic athletes to the same critical scrutiny that the pros face. "With high school sports, you can't get in someone's face and tell them, 'You blew the game,'" Luehr says. "You can't be as opinionated as you are with big-league sports. Otherwise you very quickly get parents, coaches and administrators on your back. Parents can be really sensitive."

Luehr grew up in Wisconsin and earned an English degree from the University of Wisconsin-Parkside in 1988. At Parkside he covered sports for The Ranger, the student newspaper, and eventually became sports editor. He started working for the Journal Times while still in college and has been there ever since.

A lifelong sports fan, he says the advantage of working at a local paper like the Journal Times (which has six full-time sportswriters) is that he gets to cover a bit of everything. His beat includes high school football, basketball, track, golf, swimming and, of course, soccer. He also writes columns on bowling and golf. Any aspiring sportswriter, he adds, should have that kind of broad knowledge. "Learn the basics of lots of different sports. If you work at a smaller paper you'll cover a lot of sports, and you'll need to know something about everything. It's only at the bigger papers that you become more of a specialist."

Here is Luehr's article as it appeared in the Journal Times:

MILWAUKEE—Michelle Lizotte may have been the hero for the Horlick High School girls' soccer team Saturday, but Mother Nature should get credit for a big assist.

The Rebels took advantage of a brisk tailwind in the second half to score three goals, two by Lizotte, to overcome a 2-0 deficit and beat defending WIAA Division 1 state champion Milwaukee Pius XI 3-2 at Wisconsin Lutheran High School.

With the victory, Horlick (17-6-1) will make its first WIAA State Tournament appearance since 1990. The Rebels will play Southeast Conference foe Kenosha Tremper in a quarterfinal match Thursday at 3 p.m. at Mansfield Stadium in Madison. Tremper (21-3-3) beat Horlick 2-1 in SEC play May 14. Lizotte, a sophomore forward, scored the game-tying goal with 9:37 left and the game-winner with just 31 seconds left in regulation.

"It was crazy," Lizotte said after the match. "I don't know what to say; [it was] overwhelming."

"We didn't want to go to overtime," said a jubilant Horlick coach Jim Demetriou. "In overtime, it's anybody's ballgame. The girls told me 'we don't want to go home, we want to go to state,' and we're going to state."

The Rebels appeared to be in a pretty big hole against the Lady Popes, who won nine WISAA titles and played in 12 of 14 WISAA title games before winning their first WIAA title last year. Pius had been to either the WISAA or WIAA state tournament for 13 straight years.

Pius went ahead 2-0 with 30:16 left in regulation after Courtney Grassl redirected Carly Stojsavljevic's crossing pass past Horlick goalkeeper Jen Johnson. Julia LaBlanc scored the first goal of the match for the Lady Popes in the 15th minute of the first half.

Pius had an apparent goal disallowed with 6:45 left in the first half after being offsides and had a good opportunity just a few minutes later on a hard shot by Maria Quesada, but Johnson tipped the ball so it hit high on the crossbar.

Pius had the wind in the first half and had the ball deep in Horlick's end, but could manage only the one goal.

"I felt like we played attractive soccer," said first-year Pius coach Joe Luedtke. "We had the better of possession through the whole game, but soccer is a game driven by emotion, too. They captured the emotion in the last 15 minutes and that took them to three goals."

The tailwind played right into the Rebels' style of sending long passes downfield and letting their quick forwards get to the balls and score. Their first goal didn't come that way, but that got Horlick started.

Freshman midfielder/forward Jenna Clausen stole the ball near midfield and sent a nice pass downfield to midfielder Theresa Buck. She dribbled a little bit and drove the ball high past Pius goalkeeper Meghan Ibar.

"I was just running down and Jenna passed it to me," Buck said. "It was a perfect pass, right to the middle."

Buck had another chance two minutes later, but her shot went wide. The long ball came into play inside 10 minutes left in regulation. Johnson's punt came downfield and Lizotte and junior midfielder Sam Falcone had a 2-on-1 on a Pius defender. Lizotte dribbled the ball, passed it to Falcone and she sent it back to Lizotte for a low shot past Ibar.

The teams traded possessions for the next several minutes, but the Rebels kept the pressure on Ibar. She had to dive to stop Buck's shot at 2:48 and she handled Lizotte's hard shot with 1:55. Pius got a free kick with 50 seconds left, but the Rebels got control of the ball and set up the final shot.

Buck sent a long ball to Lizotte, who beat her defender, then forced Ibar to come out before dribbling around the goalkeeper and rolling in the winning goal.

"Once they captured the momentum, they started bringing people through the middle and we didn't catch on to that quick enough," Luedtke said. "Their style caught us off guard."

One key adjustment seemed to get the Rebels going. In the final 10 minutes, Demetriou moved stopper Erin Cook to the midfield and played with three defenders across the back.

"We never gave up," said Demetriou, who with assistant coach Jeff Levonian got the traditional water shower. "We missed a lot of opportunities, but they missed a lot of opportunities."

"The girls did a fantastic job, from the back to the front," Demetriou added. "Everybody moved and everybody did their jobs."

"We came in and we wanted it more than they did," Lizotte said. "We wanted it real bad. We were like, they're not going to send us packing. They've gone to state the last 13 years and we're not going to back down."

Reprinted with permission from the Racine Journal Times.

INTERNET EXERCISES

Frank Deford is a superb sportswriter, novelist and commentator. An archive of his "Sports Illustrated" columns can be found at: **http://sportsillustrated.cnn.com/ inside_game/archives/frank_deford/**.

Philadelphia Inquirer sports columnist Bill Lyon is one of the best sportswriters—or just writers, period—working in newspapers today. You can find his work at **http://www.philly.com/mld/inquirer/sports/**.

As mentioned at the start of this chapter, many sports stories, especially those found in larger papers, are increasingly written in a feature-oriented style. Try logging onto the sports section of a big daily paper. Find a game story, and if it's written in a "featurey" style, rewrite it in a straight-sports format. Here are links to the sports sections of some major metropolitan daily papers:

The New York Times: **http://www.nytimes.com/pages/sports/index.html**

The Washington Post: **http://www.washingtonpost.com/wp-dyn/sports/**

The Miami Herald: **http://www.miami.com/mld/miamiherald/sports/**

The Philadelphia Daily News: **http://www.philly.com/mld/dailynews/sports/**

Chicago Tribune: **http://chicagosports.chicagotribune.com/**

The Houston Chronicle: **http://www.chron.com/content/chronicle/sports/**

BEYOND THE CLASSROOM

Attend a sporting event that is likely to be covered by your local newspaper. It could be a game at the high school, college or professional level. Write a story immediately after the game is over, then compare your story with the one that appears in your local paper.

Business

*t*he activities of the business world and the fluctuations of the economy affect virtually every aspect of our lives, from the price we pay for a gallon of gas to the size of our paychecks to the kinds of foods we find in the supermarket to the quality of the air we breathe. Just think about how many times each day you pull out your wallet to buy something, or write a check to pay a bill. Multiply that by a week, a month and then a year, and you get the idea. Every time you punch the clock at your job, make a bank deposit or pay taxes, you are participating in the national economy.

Yet there was a time not so long ago when many newspapers relegated business and economic stories to a page or two at the back of the news section. No more. Today business news is considered one of the most important parts of any paper, and even small local papers now typically feature a separate section on business and finance. The number of business publications has skyrocketed, and there are even entire TV networks devoted exclusively to business reporting.

There are good reasons for this increased attention. Not so long ago, relatively few Americans owned stocks (just 23 percent in 1989), and the activities of Wall Street were of interest mostly to an insider's world of corporate CEOs, stockbrokers and financial analysts. Now, with the rise of mutual funds and 401K plans, roughly half of all Americans are invested in the stock market, and that number continues to rise. It's not surprising that, as more people participate in the economy in a direct way, interest in business journalism his risen.

There are other reasons business reporting has become, well, big business. In the late 1990s U.S. economic growth exploded, fueled by the rise of high-tech companies creating everything from personal computers and software to e-commerce Web sites. As computer geeks became teenage billionaires and dot-com start-ups became, on paper at least, giant corporations almost overnight, the public's imagination was captured by the mania of what amounted to a new gold rush. And with the stock market soaring to unprecedented heights, more Americans than ever felt that, by investing wisely, they too could get a piece of the action.

In other words, the economy had become, in so many ways, one heck of a story. "With the stock boom and the economy doing well in the 1990s, and with more people owning stocks and having 401ks, there was just more interest in business news," says Getahn Ward, a business reporter with the Nashville Tennessean.

But, as is usually the case, boom was followed by bust. As the 20th century turned into the 21st, dot-com companies started to go belly up by the dozens, the bull market became a bear, and an economy that had seemed to promise limitless growth suddenly landed with a thud. Corporate scandals, bankruptcies and layoffs filled the business pages. The good times were over, at least for the time being.

But interest in business news has remained high and will likely continue to do so, says Ward, simply because business affects us all in so many ways. "It affects our everyday lives. When we buy things, when we invest, when we use services, we're interacting with the economy. It affects everyone."

KEYS TO BUSINESS COVERAGE

There are several keys to covering the business beat. First, while reporters working for specialized business publications can incorporate some business jargon into their stories, journalists writing for mass-market newspapers must be able to translate technical business terms into plain English that readers can understand. "You have to put information into simple terms," says Ward. "Business people know the language of business. They go off talking in that lingo. When you're doing an interview, you have to remind them that we're writing for a mass audience. Make them put things in laymen's terms."

Obviously, to be able to translate such terminology, one must first understand it. (A glossary of basic business terms is found later in this chapter.) A business reporter must have a solid grasp of the fundamentals of the business world, and must, on a daily basis, keep abreast of important developments in business and the economy. The Wall Street Journal, the nation's preeminent business newspaper, is required reading for business journalists from coast to coast. Business reporters who cover specific areas—high-tech industries, for example—also read specialized industry and trade publications that chronicle the doings of those kinds of businesses. "You have to stay on top of your beat," says Ward, who, in addition to his journalism training, has an M.B.A. degree. "You write for average readers, but business readers judge you on how well you understand the business world. You have to find a fine line between the two to maintain your credibility."

DON'T BELIEVE THE HYPE

Business reporters must also be wary of public relations hype. Corporations, especially large ones, are exceedingly image-conscious. They often have huge staffs devoted to putting the right "spin" on any corporate news. It's a journalist's job to sort out the real news from the company propaganda. For instance, Company X may say it is committed to a clean environment, but when Company X is found to be dumping toxic waste into a stream, a good reporter aggressively questions that commitment and separates the reality from the empty promises.

Perhaps most important, a good business reporter always remembers that business stories are *people* stories. Because the economy affects all of us in very real ways, economic fluctuations and corporate decision-making can have profound implications for millions of people. It's not enough to report that Company X has laid off 10,000 workers. The good business reporter seeks out some of those workers and interviews them in order to put a human face on the numbers. "Always keep the reader in mind," Ward advises. "At the end of the day, the goal is to get people to read the story. If you approach the story with the reader in mind, you get a better reception. I tell people how events will affect them on an individual level. You want to write your story in a balanced way that informs the reader and raises attention to the issues, but also takes into consideration how business operates."

A WIDE RANGE OF STORIES

Business reporting encompasses a huge range and variety of stories. At the most basic level are deadline stories about breaking-news developments in business and the economy—how the stock market did on a given day, what new economic forecasts are showing, and the profits or losses reported by companies in their quarterly reports. These reports, also called earnings reports, are a staple of business journalism. The key figures to look for are net income, which shows how much profit the company is making, and the earnings per share, which represents the company's total earnings divided by the number of outstanding shares. The figures are typically compared to those from the same quarter in the previous year. Here is a first-quarter earnings report from Morry's Muffin Corporation.

	2003	2002	% CHANGE
Sales	$4,305,612	$3,908,415	+10.2
Revenue	2,100,418	1,815,211	+15.7
Net Income	708,299	611,203	+15.9
Earnings Per Share	.33	.29	+13.8

Here is a story based on these figures:

Morry's Muffins Corp. said yesterday that earnings rose 15.7 percent in the first quarter, boosted by sales of the firm's new line of lowfat bran muffins.

Morry's earned $708,299, or 33 cents a share, compared to $611,203, or 29 cents a share, in the same quarter a year ago.

But business journalists must go far beyond simply reporting the latest profit-and-loss figures. They often do enterprise reporting on everything from trends in the labor market and personal finance to stories about new companies and hot new products, plant openings and closings and new construction projects. It's a big, challenging beat.

GLOSSARY OF BASIC BUSINESS TERMS

Annual Report   A detailed report on a company's finances

Asset   Stock, resources or property owned by a company

Balance Sheet   A statement showing a company's assets and liabilities

Bankruptcy   The state or condition of a person or company that liquidates its assets to pay creditors

Bear Market   A falling stock market in which more stocks are being sold than being bought

Bull Market   A rising stock market in which more stocks are being bought than sold

Capital   The investment required to start a company or business

Creditor   One to whom money is owed

Debtor   Company or person who owes money

Fixed Asset   An asset permanently used by a business, such as land or a building

Fixed Cost   The ongoing costs associated with operating a business, such as salaries, utilities, etc.

Gross   A total without any deductions

Liabilities   The debts owed by a company or individual

Net   The amount of money left after all deductions have been made

Net Worth   Assets minus liabilities

Revenue   Income

exercise one

Write an earnings story based on the following information. Deadline: 30 minutes.

A drug company called Felten-Bixell Inc., based in Toledo, Ohio, has just issued a report on its third-quarter profits. Third-quarter revenue was $208.9 million. Third-quarter profits rose 127 per cent to a record $75 million as revenue increased 37 percent. Net income for the quarter ending Sept. 30 amounted to 49 cents a share and compared with profit of $33.1 million or 22 cents per share a year earlier. Nine-month profit rose 79 percent to a record $190.6 million as revenue reached $549.3 million. Company President William Vanderson says profits were boosted by increased sales of anti-depressants and hypertension drugs. He says the company's U.S. sales force has established relationships with high-prescribing doctors through the promotion of these drugs.

exercise two

Write a story based on the following information. Deadline: 40 minutes.

Thomas Carroll, a visiting economics professor from Centerville State University, is speaking to the local Rotary Club at a luncheon at the Excelsior Hotel. His topic: The Nation's Economic Outlook Over the Next 12–18 Months. Here are some notes from his speech.

"The economic outlook is improving. After more than a year of recession, a number of economic indicators are up." He says that earlier this week, the U.S. Labor Department reported that last month's jobless rate dropped to 5.5 percent after businesses added 66,000 jobs. He also says the number of people applying for unemployment compensation has dropped for the past two months. Also, the Commerce Department reported that orders to U.S. factories for big-ticket goods rose 1.5 percent in February, the third straight monthly increase. "When businesses are adding jobs, that can only mean good news for the economy," he says. "American workers who thought they had reached a dead end during the recession are now finding that there are jobs out there."

Carroll also notes that the New York-based Conference Board announced yesterday that its Consumer Confidence Index rose to 110.2 this month from a revised 95.0 last month. Analysts had been expecting a reading of 98. He says that's the highest level in seven months. Carroll says the index is based on a monthly survey of about 5,000 U.S. households. He says it's closely watched because consumer confidence drives consumer spending, which accounts for about two-thirds of the nation's economic activity. "The improved employment picture is boosting consumer confidence in the economy," he says.

Carroll also states that while the economy appears to be growing, there are few signs of inflation, which is sometimes triggered by an expanding economy. Gas prices nationwide are down 2 percent from this time a year ago, he says.

exercise three

Write a story based on the following information. Deadline: 45 minutes.

You're a business reporter for the Havre Daily News in Montana. You've been assigned to write about the closing this week of Corral West Ranchwear, a clothing chain store in the Holiday Village Shopping Center. Here are your notes.

Chain was established in 1951; it operates 95 locations throughout the Western states. The Havre store is closing because it wasn't making enough money, regional manager Dave Denson says. "We've been here for about 10 years, and although our business has been pretty good here, we've never made a profit." He adds that the decision to close was made several months ago. The Havre store's merchandise and displays are being shipped to the Corral West store in El Paso, Texas. Fred Griffith, senior vice president of real estate for Security National, the company that owns the mall, won't say what will replace Corral West or which stores have expressed interest in filling the vacant slot.

The store has six employees, including manager Patti Schwan. She says they learned just this week they would lose their jobs. "They gave us five whole days' notice," Schwan says. "I'm not sure what I'll do now. I have no idea until something else comes along." Schwan says she and the other employees were not offered positions at the El Paso outlet. "Business was slow. The last year was really slow because of the drought," she says. "And that's my business—ranchers and farmers." She adds, "[Denson] said our store never made money. But I don't think that's right."

exercise four

Write a story based on this press release from the Securities and Exchange Commission. Deadline: one hour.

Washington, D.C., June 12, 2002—The Securities and Exchange Commission today filed charges against Samuel Waksal, the former CEO of ImClone Systems Inc., for illegal insider trading. In its complaint, the Commission charges that Waksal received disappointing news late last December that the U.S. Food and Drug Administration would soon issue a decision rejecting for review ImClone's pending application to market its cancer treatment drug, Erbitux. The SEC further charges that Waksal told this negative information to certain family members, who sold ImClone stock before the news became public and that Waksal himself tried to sell shares of ImClone before the news became public.

In its lawsuit, filed in federal court in Manhattan, the Commission seeks an order requiring that Waksal disgorge the several million dollars in losses avoided by those family members he tipped, and that he pay civil penalties and prejudgment interest. It also seeks an order permanently enjoining Waksal from violating the securities laws and barring him from acting as an officer or director of a public company.

Specifically, the Commission's complaint alleges as follows.

■ On the evening of Dec. 26, 2001, Waksal learned that on Dec. 28, 2001, the FDA would issue a Refusal to File (RTF) letter to ImClone rejecting consideration of its Biologics Licensing Application for Erbitux.
■ The same evening and early the next morning, Waksal called certain family members to alert them that ImClone would be receiving this bad news.
■ As soon as the market opened the next morning, Dec. 27, these family members sold more than $9 million of ImClone stock. In total they sold more than $10 million of ImClone stock over the next two days.
■ Also starting that evening, Dec. 26, and through Dec. 28, Waksal himself tried to sell 79,797 shares of ImClone stock worth nearly $5 million. He was unable to do so only because two different broker-dealers would not execute the orders.
■ As expected, the FDA faxed ImClone the RTF letter at about 4 p.m. on Dec. 28, 2001. At 6 p.m. that day, ImClone publicly announced the FDA decision. By the close of trading on Dec. 31, the next trading day, ImClone's stock price had dropped 16 percent, from $55.25 to $46.46.
■ By selling before the announcement that ImClone had received an RTF letter from the FDA, Waksal family members avoided losses of several million dollars.

The Commission's complaint alleges that based on this conduct, Waksal violated Section 17(a) of the Securities Act of 1933 and Section 10(b) of the Securities Exchange Act of 1934 and Rule 10b-5 thereunder. The Commission's investigation is ongoing. The Commission acknowledges the assistance of the U.S. Attorney's Office for the Southern District of New York in the investigation of this matter.

Real REPORTER: Getahn Ward

It was a story some reporters might pass over as too complex or even dull. Bank of America was suing the state of Tennessee over an obscure state law involving the cashing of checks. But Getahn Ward, a business reporter for the Nashville Tennessean, understood the real implications of the story: if Bank of America won its lawsuit, many state residents would have to pay a fee for simply trying to cash checks at Bank of America branches. Ward approached the story from this angle; indeed, that's how he handles every story on his beat. "I want to tell people how business affects them on an individual level. You should always keep your reader in mind."

Ward discovered the story when he was making his regular weekly check of lawsuits filed in the federal court in Nashville. (Many reporters find that their beats cross paths with other beats. For instance, police reporters often have to check court documents, or court reporters may need to check police records.) In a nutshell, Bank of America's lawsuit was asking a federal judge in Nashville to overturn a state law that barred banks from charging fees to cash payroll and other checks written by their own customers. The bank said it wanted to be able to charge noncustomers to cash checks issued by its business clients.

Bank of America (and other banks for that matter) had filed similar suits in other states. Ward kept abreast of those suits, so he was somewhat familiar with the issue. But he knew he needed to wade through the legalese of the court documents to make sure he grasped exactly what the suit was about. Then he needed to quickly write a lead for the story because his editor was going into an afternoon news meeting and needed to be able to tell other editors what the story was about. Reporters often have to write a lead, or what's sometimes called a budget line, for a story early in the day. That budget line is used by editors in news meetings and also put on the daily news digest, or budget—a list of all the major stories going into that day's paper.

Having written a line for the news budget, Ward knew he needed more than just the substance of the lawsuit itself for his story. He needed to get quotes from those involved in the suit (the state and the bank), and he needed to talk to groups that would oppose such fees. "I tried to talk to the bank and to the other parties involved, to get some insight as to what this would mean to them. Because this was really a consumer story, I needed to talk to some consumer groups also. As I started gathering the information I began, little by little, to pull the pieces together," he adds. "I had to wait to get people to call me back, and I was also working on some other stories at the same time."

In other words, it was a fairly typical day for Ward—and for most journalists, for that matter. It's rare for a newspaper reporter to have the luxury of just working on one story at a time. Usually, he's juggling several different articles—some due within hours or minutes, others due in several days.

Ward spent about three hours reporting the lawsuit story, and maybe an hour or so writing it. That's also fairly typical—most reporters spend about twice as much time gathering information and doing interviews as they do writing. And often, the writing is done in stages, as material for the story is gathered. "When you're writing on deadline, you have to think the story through even as you're reporting it. Once I know the theme of the story I don't need all the information to start writing. I can write the first few paragraphs, and then as I go along I gradually fill in the holes."

With the Bank of America story, "I thought it was important to tell people early on in the story what this lawsuit would mean to them." Ward's lead did just that, clearly and succinctly: *If Bank of America gets its way, noncustomers statewide who visit branch locations to cash checks drawn on the bank could face a $5 fee.*

Ward grew up in the African nation of Liberia, and at an early age started writing poetry and short stories. He was an intern at a paper there and dreamed of making a career in journalism, but a civil war forced him to leave his homeland in 1991. He came to the United States and decided to study business, earning his bachelor's degree and an M.B.A. from Tennessee State University. But his love of writing never waned; he wrote for the campus paper and did a summer internship at The Commercial Appeal newspaper in Memphis. Eventually he landed a part-time business reporting job at the Nashville Banner, and when that paper folded in 1998, he was hired as a full-time reporter at the Nashville Tennessean, where he covers financial services and public companies.

Here is the story Ward wrote about the Bank of America lawsuit.

If Bank of America gets its way, noncustomers statewide who visit branch locations to cash checks drawn on the bank could face a $5 fee.

The bank has sued Tennessee, asking a federal judge in Nashville to declare void a state law that bars banks from charging fees to cash payroll and other checks. Bank of America, specifically, said it wants to charge noncustomers to cash checks issued by its business clients.

The lawsuit marks the latest in efforts by the banking industry to reduce the check-cashing lines in branches while gaining additional business and fees.

Last December, Bank of America, Wells Fargo and other banks won a ruling against a similar Texas law. An appeal is pending. In June, Bank of America filed a similar suit against Georgia.

Bank of America hasn't said how much it would charge here if it wins the case. The bank, however, charges $5 to cash noncustomers' checks in Arizona, Florida, Nevada, New Mexico, the Carolinas and Texas, bank spokesman Harvey Radin said.

Typically, banks charge noncustomers for cashing checks drawn on other banks. Tennessee is among a handful of states that prohibit collecting fees for cashing checks drawn on that bank.

Consumer advocates see the legal challenges as part of efforts by large banks to make it harder for people to access their money.

"Bank of America always advertises that it's consumer-friendly and this lawsuit is anything but that," said Jill Johnson, Southern field organizer with the U.S. Public Interest Research Group of Washington, D.C.

Radin, who is based in San Francisco, sees it differently.

"It's really about our rights to price our products and services," he said about the Nashville suit filed last week.

In its suit, the Charlotte, N.C.-based Bank of America argues that the 1970 state law violates the rights of banks under a national banking act to price their services and that federal law preempts the state statute.

The federal law specifically applies to national banks.

Radin said banks incur much cost in cashing checks for noncustomers and doing so affects service to customers. Noncustomers have options such as using their own bank or setting up a no-fee direct deposit account, he said.

The lawsuit identifies Fred R. Lawson, commissioner of the state's financial institutions department, as the defendant. Besides a permanent injunction, the suit seeks payment of attorneys' fees.

Michael E. Moore, an attorney at the attorney general's office, referred calls to a spokeswoman for the office who could not be reached.

Bank of America has the third-largest market share in the Nashville area and has 90 branches statewide.

Copyrighted by The Tennessean, August 6, 2002.

INTERNET EXERCISES

The Securities and Exchange Commission requires all public companies (except foreign companies and companies with less than $10 million in assets and 500 shareholders) to file registration statements, periodic reports, and other forms. Those forms, which can be used as the basis for news stories, can be accessed online at **http://www.sec.gov/edgar. shtml**. In addition, press releases issued by the SEC about its enforcement actions can be found at **http://www.sec.gov/news/press.shtml**.

Press releases issued by corporations can be used as the basis for newswriting exercises, as long as you are able to separate the fact from the public relations hogwash. Here are a few Web sites where such releases, including quarterly earnings reports, can be found:

P.R. Newswire   **http://www.prnewswire.com/**

Business Wire   **http://www.businesswire.com/**

In-Stat MDR   **http://www.instat.com/ebusiness.asp**

BEYOND THE CLASSROOM

Make an appointment to visit a local company in your area. Ask to see their latest quarterly report, and interview one of the company's executives about the fiscal health of the firm. Write a story based on the information you gather.

Obituaries

*O*bituaries are written when someone dies, yet they are really a celebration of a person's life. They follow a relatively simple format, but, in the hands of a pro, can be an example of beautiful writing. They are sometimes scorned by reporters as busy work, yet are one of the most widely read features in any newspaper. And for the beginning reporter, the ability to write a compelling obit is as essential as being able to cover cops or courts.

There are really two kinds of obituaries. One is a routine recitation of basic details of the deceased person's life. It includes name, age, occupation, and home address; circumstances of the death; details of their funeral and burial plans; and names of any surviving family members. This type of obit, sometimes called a death notice, is often provided to newspapers by mortuaries. Here's the lead from a death-notice obit:

> *Philip Longo, age 90, of Bensalem, Pa., passed away Monday, June 12, at Manahawkin Nursing and Rehabilitation Center.*
>
> *Born in Levittown, he resided in Croydon and Northeast Philadelphia before moving to Bensalem in 1992.*

You get the idea. The facts are there, but it makes for pretty dry reading. This kind of obit is most frequently found in small, short-staffed newspapers that can't afford a full-time obit writer.

The second type of obituary is sometimes called the biographical obit. It provides all the facts found in a death notice, but goes further, providing a rich and detailed account of the person's life in a way that a death notice could never match. This chapter discusses the biographical obit.

Contrast the lead above with the one below by Jere Hester of the New York Daily News.

> *Fans around the world mourned yesterday for George Harrison, whose crisp guitar solos, sweet harmony vocals and songwriting prowess helped make the Beatles the most successful pop group ever.*
>
> *The youngest member of the Fab Four, known as much for his droll wit as his deep spiritualism, lost his battle with cancer Thursday afternoon. He was 58.*

You see the difference. The first lead is dull. The second is interesting. The first lead recites facts. The second begins to paint a picture of the person. The first is written almost mechanically. The second is written with style.

The lead of a biographical obit generally includes several key elements: the name of the deceased, the age, the circumstances of death and, perhaps most important, a summary of what made the person's life remarkable, interesting, unusual or unique. Here's another example:

> *Janet Washington, a jazz pianist who entertained audiences in the Philadelphia area for more than four decades with her bluesy, soulful style of playing, died Sunday after a long battle with cancer. She was 87.*

You see how this lead manages to combine hard information—name, age, circumstances of death—with a passage that gives the reader a sense of what her life was all about—music.

The leads of biographical obits generally follow this format if the deceased is elderly or has been ill—in other words, if his or her death is not a surprise. But if the deceased's death is unexpected—if he or she is young, for instance, or dies as the result of an accident, unusual illness or foul play—then the lead should include greater detail on the circumstances of death. Here's an example of this kind of lead:

> *Jim Kozlowski, Centerville High School football coach for the last 11 years, collapsed during a practice yesterday and was rushed to County General Hospital, where he was pronounced dead of a heart attack. He was 36.*
>
> *Kozlowski had had no history of heart problems, said his wife, Angie. He was a dedicated jogger who sometimes ran 4 miles a day, she said.*

Kozlowski was known as a tough but warm coach who had earned the respect and admiration of his players over the years.

The coach was young and seemingly healthy, so when he dies of a heart attack it merits greater detail at the top of the story.

The body of the obit should elaborate on its lead. It should include basic biographical data about the person: where they were born and grew up, details of their education, military service, career, marriage, family and so on. But it should always return to the focus established in the lead, the thing that made the person's life unique from all others.

Hester, who has written obituaries of Richard Nixon, Supreme Court Justice Harry Blackmun, Jimmy Stewart and Jacqueline Kennedy Onassis, among others, says a good obit is a combination of facts and colorful, telling details. "You want to have the cradle-to-grave biographical information in there, but you also want to imbue the story with what made this person special, why they were important, what their contribution was. You're dealing with facts but you don't want a dull recitation of facts."

"Everybody's life is worth telling, whether it' someone who's lived an exemplary life, like Mother Teresa, or someone who's led a less than exemplary life, like [New York mobster] John Gotti. I think there's something inherently interesting in everyone's story. When you see all the lives lost in the Sept. 11 terror attacks, every one of those lives was worth a story."

QUICK TIPS

- Obit leads generally include the name and age of the deceased, the circumstances of death and a summary of what made this life unique.

- If the deceased's death is unexpected, the lead should include greater detail on the circumstances of death.

exercise one

Write an obit based on the following notes. Deadline: 45 minutes.

Henry Washington, principal at Pennsbury High, says, "Annette taught thousands of students over the years, and I think they all loved her. She managed to not only make high school geometry, trigonometry and calculus interesting, she made it fun. That's not easy. She had an engaging teaching style; she loved to joke with her students." Diane Martin, 40, who teaches math at Pennsbury, was once a student of Nelson's. She says, "Annette inspired me to become a math teacher. She was kind of a mentor to me. She was fun, but she was tough, too. I learned so much from her."

Annette Lynn Nelson, age 80, died on Friday, June 28, at Doylestown Hospital; had cancer the last several years. Born Annette Lynn Whitcover in Springfield, Ma., she moved to Bensalem, Pa., with her family when she was young; graduated from Bensalem High School; attended the University of Pennsylvania, got bachelor's degree in mathematics in 1942. Taught in the Philadelphia school system for several years before moving to Fairless Hills to teach at Pennsbury High School. In 1951 she married Jack Nelson, editor of several weekly community newspapers in the area. They were married 45 years; he died in 1996. She taught at Pennsbury High for 42 years; retired in 1987. Nelson is survived by two sons, Jack Jr. and Thomas; and three grandchildren. Viewing will be 7 p.m. Friday in the Lincoln Funeral Home, 3700 Brookline St. in Fairless Hills.

exercise two

You're a reporter for the Centurion, the student newspaper at Bucks County Community College. Jennifer Lynn Mocarski, a student at the college, has died. Write an obit based on your notes from interviews with family and friends. Deadline: one hour.

Susan Darrah, chair of the Language and Literature Department at Bucks, had Mocarski in one of her women's studies distance learning classes. Darrah says, "She was my best student. Jenny was a smart kid and a fine writer." Mocarski's mom tells you, "Jenny touched many people's lives. It was like a rally when people found out [she died]. She had a friend come up from Georgia and 10 from Virginia. Jenny was a loving, caring person. My daughter was amazing."

Mocarski, 21, from Bensalem, known as Jenny to family; graduated from Bensalem High School in 1997; was a student in the gifted program and a member of the community service club, student government and the debate team; attended Mary Washington College in Fredericksburg, Va., majoring in journalism. But she suffered from a rare spinal disorder; as the disease got worse she had to leave Mary Washington and return home to Bensalem. She enrolled at Bucks, took distance learning courses, wanted to earn her associate's degree.

Jenny's mom, Patricia Mocarski, tells you her daughter suffered from rigid spinal syndrome, which limits mobility by making leg muscles stiff and nearly inflexible; it also restricts airflow to the lungs. Mocarski's symptoms first appeared at age 12 or 13 when she had trouble with flexibility during dance classes, which she took for eight years. The illness went undiagnosed for years; finally Dr. Donald Schotland, a neuromuscular specialist at the University of Pennsylvania, diagnosed rigid spinal syndrome last year. Disease is incurable. Mocarski was scheduled to fly to England next month to meet Dr. Victor Dubowitz for a three-day evaluation. Dubowitz wanted to verify the disease and make recommendations for treatment.

Patricia Mocarski tells you Jenny was taken to a local hospital the day before she died; she was complaining of a popping sound in her ears and difficulty sleeping; doctor gave Mocarski sleeping pills and sent her home. Jenny had been losing weight and recently began to use crutches to walk. Mrs. Mocarski says the disease apparently caused Jenny to stop breathing. She tells you: "It was as if she knew. Before she went to bed Sunday night she told me not to be sad. I said 'good night' to her, and I was returning downstairs when she called for me to come back to her room. She wanted to give me a hug and tell me that she loved me. Then she called for my husband, and told him the same. I went to check on her about 45 minutes later. She had stopped breathing."

exercise three

You're a reporter for the Centurion, the student newspaper of Bucks County Community College. James Daniel Joseph Murphy Bock, a 20-year-old graphic arts major at the college, has died. Write an obit based on the following notes from interviews with his friends and family. Deadline: 75 minutes.

Bock was born on Oct. 8, 1981, in Philadelphia; family later moved to Langhorne; graduated from Archbishop Wood High School in 1999, attended East Stroudsburg University majoring in education. hosted a radio show called "Lunch With Bob," after Bob Dylan, his favorite musician; began collecting Dylan's records when he was in high school; had attended at least six Dylan concerts. For one show he drove 11 hours to Charlotte, N.C., watched the show and then drove straight back home. He was also going to attend a Dylan concert next month in Wake Forest, N.C.; a prized possession was a rare 1975 Bob Dylan vinyl he had just bought on the Internet for $6. His mother tells you, "I asked Jim how much it was and I was thinking he was gonna say $100, he told me it would be somewhere around $10 so I said go for it." Justin Gajeway, his best friend, tells you, "He listened to the record once, burned it on a CD and then put it back on his wall."

Bock was from Langhorne; he leaves behind his parents James and Patricia, sister Jessica, his girlfriend Tracy Ann Franklin, 20, and Justin Gajeway, 20. The viewing was held at the new St. Andrew's church in Newtown; he was buried in Our Lady of Sorrows cemetery in Langhorne; funeral was attended by more than 300 people.

Bock met Franklin at Stroudsburg. After two semesters, he left and started attending Bucks County Community College; he changed his major to graphic arts. This was his third semester at Bucks; he had a 3.0 GPA. "For once in his life Jim was worried about his cumulative grade point average," his father tells you.

Bock loved hiking and the outdoors. He had been a Boy Scout; earned the rank of Eagle Scout when he was 15, the youngest ever to attain that rank in his troop. He had hiked the Long Trail in Vermont and the Northville Placid trail in New York. For his senior week trip he and Gajeway tried to hike the entire Pennsylvania portion of the Appalachian Trail.

Bock was aspiring poet and artist. This past Christmas he put together a book of his poetry, gave copies to friends; had one of his artworks on display last spring at the Bucks art show.

Quote from mom: "Right after we moved to Langhorne I started working full-time and we allowed Jim and Jessica to stay home alone. I came home one night and I see the window open with a rope coming in the window. I asked Jim what was going on and it turned out he and his sister were attempting to catch pigeons."

Gajeway tells you Bock was a great big brother to his sister. They were both born on the same day three years apart. His mom felt there was a cosmic connection between the two, who were always hanging out together growing up.

"I was amazed, they were the only brother and sister I knew that got along perfectly," Gajeway says.

His mother tells you he was a great son. "The one thing I wanted every year was a picture of the kids with Santa. Jim really fought me on it this year saying, 'This is the last year I am doing it, I am gonna be 21 next year so this is it' but he went and got a Santa picture with his sister for mom," she says.

Bock's girlfriend tells you they met at Stroudsburg during their second semester. The first night they spent together was on Super Bowl Sunday but they played chess all night. They attended several Dylan shows together and went hiking on the Appalachian Trail twice. "We always said we had a romantic side, but we acted like best friends. Most of the time we would just hang out and watch movies or cartoons," she says.

Bock's family tells you he died of a brain aneurysm. The day he died, Bock felt sick in class and came home to lie down. His sister went into his room later in the afternoon to get him up for work and saw something was wrong. She called 911 but it was too late. Gajeway says he had called him earlier in the day to make plans for the evening. "I remember looking at the clock on my computer and it was 3:56 p.m., I asked his sister to wake him up and she said Jim said he would call me back." His family says Bock had no previous medical history that would have led to his sudden death. "He was a good all-around kid who had a bright future ahead of him, unfortunately he had a terrible aneurysm," his father tells you.

Real REPORTER: Jere Hester

As word spread in the fall of 2001 that George Harrison was waging a life-and-death battle with cancer, news organizations worldwide began writing obituaries for the former Beatle.

To a nonjournalist, the idea of preparing a story about the death of a person who is still alive can sound ghoulish. But in the world of breaking news, when minutes count, such preparations are crucial. That's because obits—especially those for people deemed newsworthy—can run several thousand words. They take time to write. And if news of the person's death breaks close to deadline, news organizations need a story they can get into the paper, onto the wires or posted at a Web site quickly.

In fact, many of the largest newspapers, and certainly the major wire services, have dozens of obituaries at the ready for personalities ranging from major world leaders to athletes and movie stars. At the New York Daily News, night city editor Jere Hester, a lifelong Beatles fan, began assembling a Harrison obit in late November. "We had been hearing reports and rumors about his health for weeks," Hester recalls. "Our sources were telling us he was in worse shape than we'd been led to believe in the press."

Hester spent several hours poring over background clips and books about Harrison. He also culled information from Lexis-Nexis, an online database many reporters use that contains thousands of newspaper articles from years past. Using that material, Hester began to write the first draft of a Harrison obit. "Obviously this was someone who merited special attention. I started to write, and at that point, when he hadn't died yet, there was less of a feeling of urgency. But those are the best times to do your serious research, to map out what you should include and what additional research you should do."

Indeed, with a personality like Harrison, there was a seemingly endless amount of background data. Hester found that deciding what to leave out of the obit was a major task. "I probably spent about 20 percent of my time writing and the other 80 percent cutting and rewriting," he says. "You know you can't get everything in, but there's going to be something that if you leave it out, you know you won't be able to sleep that night. You have to say a lot in a few words. With someone like this it's a particular challenge."

Hester wrote the obit in about two hours. Several days later, on the morning of Friday, Nov. 30, news flashed across the globe that Harrison had died. Even though Hester's first draft was written—"in the can," as journalists put it—his work was only beginning. Reaction to Harrison's death was global. The remaining Beatles and a host of rock 'n' roll luminaries issued statements. Fans congregated at Beatles landmarks like Abbey Road studios in London. In New York, mourners massed in Strawberry Fields, a patch of Central Park dedicated to Harrison's slain bandmate, John Lennon. Even British Prime Minister Tony Blair and President George Bush had something to say about Harrison's passing.

Elements of all these things had to be worked into the obit. "You can have all the facts laid out, but sometimes the spark that needs to go into a story like this doesn't hit you until the person dies," Hester says. "You see people worldwide reacting to this, and it makes you rethink the story. The fresh thing is the reaction. It takes the facts you've written and puts life into them."

Hester raced to the newsroom that morning "and did a writethru on the story from beginning to end. I added things throughout the day as more reaction came in. That meant sentences and whole paragraphs had to undergo overhauls." The overhauls had to be done quickly. As a Daily News editor, Hester also had to help coordinate a large package of stories about Harrison for the next day's paper. Between all of his other work that day, Hester estimates he spent about two hours writing the final version of the Harrison obit. "With an obit like this, you're writing for a number of audiences. You have to make it ring true to the people who were there when Beatlemania happened. You're going to bring back a memory. But you also have to think about people to whom Harrison was just a name or a face, and try to get across why this person was important and special in their time," he adds. "Maybe they'll get it and maybe they won't. You want them to feel some excitement. You want them to maybe go to their parents and ask, 'did you watch Ed Sullivan the night the Beatles were on?'"

Hester, a lifelong Brooklyn resident, says he's read newspapers since he was a kid, "and the Daily News was always the one at the top of the pile." He majored in politics and journalism at New York University, then worked at a string of weekly papers in Manhattan before joining the News in 1992. He started out as a general assignment reporter, but his skills as a gifted, speedy writer soon landed him on the News' legendary rewrite desk. On rewrite, Hester handled dozens of major stories, including the O.J. Simpson trial, the death of Princess Diana and the Long Island Railroad massacre. He was appointed night city editor in July 2000.

"With breaking news, you've got to write what you know as you learn it. That way, it comes across as very fresh," Hester says. "The trick, when you're on a tight deadline, is that as you're writing one sentence, you're already thinking ahead to the one after that." Hester strives to write sentences that are "clear, punchy and active. As you write a story, imagine how you would tell a friend or loved one about it. It's got to be, 'Hey, you won't believe what just happened.' That makes for good, lively conversational writing. You should want the reader to be as excited about reading your story as you are about writing it. That's what you've got to try to bring to it." Below is Hester's obituary for George Harrison.

Fans around the world mourned yesterday for George Harrison, whose crisp guitar solos, sweet harmony vocals and songwriting prowess helped make the Beatles the most successful pop group ever.

The youngest member of the Fab Four, known as much for his droll wit as his deep spiritualism, lost his battle with cancer Thursday afternoon. He was 58.

Harrison, who went from Switzerland to Staten Island in search of treatment, died at a friend's home in Los Angeles. His wife, Olivia, and son, Dhani, were by his side. "He left this world as he lived in it, conscious of God, fearless of death and at peace, surrounded by family and friends," the Harrison family said in a statement. "He often said, 'Everything else can wait, but the search for God cannot wait, and love one another.' "

Around the globe, fans gently wept yesterday, gathering from Central Park's Strawberry Fields to London's Abbey Road to sing his songs and celebrate the life of, as the people of Liverpool say, one of the "four lads who shook the world."

"We will miss George for his sense of love, his sense of music and his sense of laughter," Ringo Starr said in a statement.

"He is really, just my baby brother," a "devastated" Paul McCartney said in England.

It wasn't immediately known whether there would be a public memorial for Harrison, an ex-smoker who had battled cancer since 1997 and was stabbed by a deranged fan in 1999.

A private ceremony already had taken place, said a family friend, security expert Gavin De Becker, at whose home Harrison is said to have died.

Harrison's death, which came nearly 21 years after John Lennon was slain in New York, closed another chapter in the story of a musical and cultural phenomenon that helped define the 1960s and continues to defy generational boundaries.

Though Harrison was pegged the Quiet Beatle, his voice—he was known as the Invisible Singer for his backup vocals—and musicianship—his guitar solos were eight-bar masterpieces of flash melded with melody—were key to the group's success.

A Hit Songwriter

And while he long toiled in the shadow of the powerhouse songwriting team of Lennon and McCartney, he eventually crafted his share of classics, including "Taxman," "While My Guitar Gently Weeps," "Something" and "Here Comes the Sun."

He introduced the sitar to rock 'n' roll, and his embrace of Indian culture and the teachings of the Maharishi Mahesh Yogi is credited by some with helping to popularize yoga and transcendental meditation in the West.

His Concert for Bangladesh—the first of the mega fund-raisers—helped instill a sense of conscience and duty in rock 'n' roll. And even as he often cursed his fame and reviled the godlike status some fanatics accorded the group, for George Harrison, the meaning of the Beatles all came down to the music.

He once said, "I think people who truly can live a life in music are telling the world, 'You can have my love, you can have my smiles. Forget the bad parts, you don't need them. Just take the music, the goodness, because it's the very best, and it's the part I give most willingly.' "

Born a bus driver's son Feb. 24, 1943, in war-torn Liverpool, Harrison took up the guitar at 13, practicing until his fingertips bled, as his mother stood nearby, encouraging him.

In 1957, the part-time butcher's errand boy met fellow aspiring musician Paul McCartney, who soon introduced him to a brash pal named John Lennon.

Lennon—dismissive of Harrison, who was three years younger than him—challenged him to play "Raunchy," a popular song of the time. Harrison tore off a note-perfect version, earning a spot in Lennon's group, the Quarrymen.

In 1960, Harrison joined Lennon and McCartney in Hamburg, playing seedy clubs on the notorious Reeperbahn strip as the Silver Beatles. They'd crank out mostly American rock 'n' roll hits eight hours a night, honing their chops, popping uppers and raising hell.

They returned to Liverpool local heroes, playing to swooning teenage girls at the Cavern club on Mathew Street, providing the first microcosm of what was to become Beatlemania. They cut a few singles, scoring no success in the U.S. but hitting the British charts with songs such as "Love Me Do" and "Please Please Me."

In February 1964, three months after the assassination of President John F. Kennedy, the group suddenly exploded on the American scene, making their live U.S. TV debut on "The Ed Sullivan Show," before an audience of more than 73 million.

Girls screamed. Parents groaned. The press howled.

What do you call that haircut? reporters asked Harrison.

"Arthur," he deadpanned.

Suddenly, the group had the top five spots on the charts, teenagers were lining up for Beatle haircuts and jamming concert halls, screaming so loud the band couldn't hear themselves.

And even the critics who initially dismissed them as a fad were charmed by the Beatles' first film, "A Hard Day's Night," an ebullient Marx Brothers-like romp set to music.

It was on the movie set that Harrison met Patti Boyd, a model and actress, whom he wed in 1966.

Later that year, the Beatles, sick of playing to crowds more interested in screaming than listening, gave up touring and became strictly a studio band.

Scores On "Revolver"

For Harrison, it began his most productive Beatle years. On "Revolver," he was slotted three compositions on an album for the first time—including, "Taxman," his best yet.

Times were quickly changing, and so was the group: By now, all but Paul were married, and the moptops had given way to shoulder-length locks and facial hair. Pills and pot turned to experimentation with LSD. Collarless Edwardian suits were doffed in favor of wild, psychedelic-inspired attire.

The Beatles unofficially kicked off the Summer of Love with the release of "Sgt. Pepper's Lonely Hearts Club Band" in June 1967, the year the youth movement turned from fad to social revolution. Whether the Beatles were a cause of the vast cultural shift or just a sign of the times is debatable, but Harrison wasn't taking credit—or blame.

"The world used us as an excuse to go mad," he once said.

Harrison, like his bandmates, began experimenting with new sounds in the studio. He became a student of the sitar after picking one up on the set of the group's second movie, "Help!"

This began an obsession with Indian music and culture that took the Beatles to India in 1968, where they studied with the Maharishi Mahesh Yogi, a spiritual guru whom Lennon later blasted as a fraud.

Harrison, though, stuck with Eastern spiritualism and music, championing Indian musician Ravi Shankar and using the sitar on such songs as "Within You Without You" and "Norwegian Wood."

By the time the group returned from India, they were bickering almost constantly. Yet the foursome—particularly Harrison—thrived musically.

His songs on the group's final albums included "While My Guitar Gently Weeps," "Here Comes the Sun" and "Something," as he emerged from Lennon and McCartney's shadow.

After the group broke up in 1970, Harrison was first to release a hit single: "My Sweet Lord"—an ode to the Hare Krishna movement—off the critically acclaimed "All Things Must Pass" triple album.

He also organized the 1971 Concert for Bangladesh at Madison Square Garden, a landmark event that drew Bob Dylan, Eric Clapton and Starr.

A handful of subsequent singles did well, but by the mid-1970s, Harrison's output and popularity had diminished, as had his taste for public life.

In 1976, he was forced to pay $587,000 for "subconsciously" stealing the tune for "My Sweet Lord" from the 1963 Chiffons hit "He's So Fine."

He and Boyd divorced in 1977, after she left him for his pal, guitar great Clapton, who had long pined for her—most memorably in the song "Layla."

Soon after, Harrison wed Olivia Arias, had a son, Dhani, and took to gardening and meditating behind the walls of his massive English estate, Friar Park.

Harrison laughed off tabloid reports portraying him as a crazy, Howard Hughes-like recluse. But he clearly cherished privacy. "The nicest thing is to open the newspapers and not to find yourself in them," he once said.

He also kept busy producing movies—most notably, Monty Python's "Life of Brian"—and he liked to race cars.

What he didn't much like was the constant questions about whether the Beatles would ever reunite—especially after the 1980 slaying of Lennon.

"As far as I'm concerned, there won't be a Beatles reunion as long as John Lennon remains dead," Harrison once quipped.

Still, Lennon's death began a thaw in relations among the surviving Beatles. Harrison's "All Those Years Ago," a musical tribute to his fallen pal, was recorded with McCartney and Starr.

In the late 1980s, he had a musical rebirth with the album "Cloud Nine," featuring the hit "Got My Mind Set on You." He joined The Traveling Wilburys supergroup, and for all his problems with the Beatles, he turned up with Starr for the group's Rock and Roll Hall of Fame induction in 1988.

Harrison did a string of concerts with Clapton in Japan in 1991 and took the stage the following year at the Dylan tribute at Madison Square Garden.

In 1995, Harrison and the surviving Beatles reunited for the "Anthology" albums and documentary, completing two demos—"Free as a Bird" and "Real Love"—left behind by Lennon.

The "Anthology" albums were huge successes—as was last year's greatest hits collection, "1", which went to No. 1 in more than three dozen countries.

But for all the renewed musical triumphs, Harrison was plagued by bad health.

In 1997, Harrison, once a heavy smoker, was treated for throat cancer, and he was said to have made a full recovery.

But in December 1999, a mentally disturbed intruder broke into his English estate and stabbed Harrison in the chest with a 7-inch knife. He suffered a punctured lung but escaped with his life after his wife clubbed the attacker with a fireplace poker and a table lamp.

In May, he was treated for lung cancer, and by July there were reports the disease had spread to his brain. He was treated at a Swiss clinic over the summer and in October checked into Staten Island University Hospital for experimental fractionated stereotactic radiosurgery treatments.

McCartney and Starr reportedly visited Harrison on Staten Island, bidding him good-bye. Harrison was said to have gone to UCLA Medical Center last week for chemotherapy.

Still, he found the strength Oct. 1 to record a final song, "A Horse to Water," co-written with his 23-year-old son.

In a droll farewell joke, the publishing credit on the song reads: RIP Ltd. 2001.

New York Daily News L.P., reprinted with permission.

INTERNET EXERCISES

In the months after Sept. 11, The New York Times attempted to profile every person killed in the terrorist attacks. While not done in the traditional obit format, the Times' "Portraits of Grief" are powerfully and poignantly written, a stirring example of how every life is worth a story. "Portraits of Grief" can be found at **http://www.nytimes.com/pages/national/portraits/**.

Several Web sites offer good tips on writing obits:

- The Detroit Free Press offers tips at **http://www.freep.com/jobspage/academy/obits.htm**.
- The No Train, No Gain journalism site has helpful info at **http://www.notrain-nogain.org/Listsv/Arc/obit.asp**.

Try writing an obit for a famous person who's still alive. You can get lots of biographical data on the famous at **http://www.biography.com**, **http://www.infoplease.com**, **http://www.factmonster.com** and The Biographical Dictionary at **http://www.s9.com/biography/**.

12

Science and Medicine

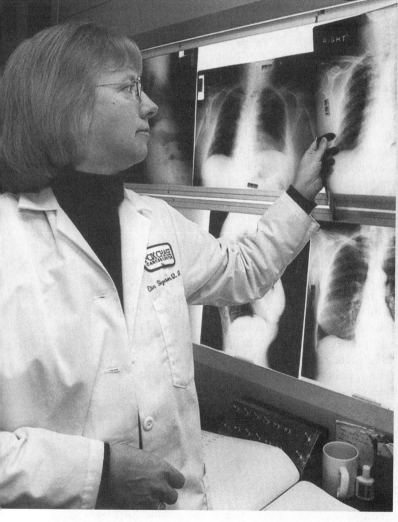

*a*sk Daniel Q. Haney why he likes covering the medical beat, and he'll give you a quick answer: "It's always changing." Haney, medical editor of The Associated Press, continues, "On a lot of beats you see the same things year after year. But science and medicine are moving very quickly. You have to work hard to keep up and stay current. It's never boring."

Indeed it's not. Science and medical reporters (and those covering related areas, like high technology or space exploration) get to write about research that's literally on the frontier of human knowledge. Whether it's the discovery of planets circling distant star systems or advances in cloning and new methods of treating age-old diseases, these beats have the power to astonish even the most jaded reader.

But they are also extraordinarily challenging beats to cover well. Science and medicine are highly specialized, complex areas of human endeavor. Researchers and physicians spend years in training just to achieve basic levels of competence in their fields. How, you might ask, can a reporter without an M.D. or Ph.D expect to write about such fields knowledgably? "It's like covering any other beat," says Haney. "You can't cover baseball without knowing the rules of the game and the nuances. If you tried to walk in and just start covering a game without knowing those things, you'd be lost. It's the same way covering medicine. You have to be quite current with the jargon and the state of advances in the field. You should know the broad outlines of the field and understand the language they use."

In other words, you must do your homework. Science and medical reporters regularly scour scientific journals, attend conferences and talk to experts in order to make their knowledge of the field as broad and as deep as possible. Of course, that doesn't mean you have to understand the subject the same way a doctor or scientist does. That wouldn't be practical or possible. But it does mean having a solid layperson's grasp of the material—solid enough to translate the information into terms that are simple enough for the average reader to understand and accurate enough to satisfy the discriminating expert.

Haney suggests doing the research "before you call up people for interviews or go to press conferences. If you're writing about heart disease and you don't know what exactly a heart attack is, you should find out first. You shouldn't have to ask a cardiologist." That saves time in the interview and allows you to ask informed questions, Haney says. "Also, you put the person you're interviewing at ease if they think you know what you're talking about. There's nothing that scares a doctor more than being interviewed by a reporter who's at sea on the topic being discussed. They think the reporter is going to screw the story up."

But scientists can screw up too, and that raises another important point for the reporter covering this beat. Be wary, especially when writing about new research, of calling a theory a fact. As any scientist will tell you, science is a process of acquiring knowledge through the painstaking, trial-and-error process of experimentation. Many scientists spend years doing research, all in an effort to prove a theory that is later shown to be wrong. Remember, at one time the world's greatest scientists believed our planet was flat. Treat research studies with a healthy dose of skepticism, and avoid using phrases like "groundbreaking" or "definitive" to describe research that's in its early stages. And do what good reporters always do—get both sides of the story. If a scientist proposes a startling new theory or claims to have made a major new discovery, chances are there will be another scientist out there to question those claims. Interview both of them for your story.

QUICK TIPS

- Make sure you thoroughly understand the material you've covering before trying to write about it.

- Do as much research as you can on your own. But once you've done that, don't be afraid to ask the experts plenty of questions.

- Keep the language as simple as possible. Avoid scientific jargon or phrases that the average reader won't understand.

- Approach new research with a healthy dose of skepticism; don't report a scientific discovery as fact until the scientific community at large has accepted it as such.
- If there is a dispute or controversy, get both sides of the issue.

exercise one

Below is an abstract (a summary of a research study) from "The New England Journal of Medicine." Rewrite it in news style. Deadline: 30 minutes.

Background The worldwide threat of arthropod-transmitted diseases, with their associated morbidity and mortality, underscores the need for effective insect repellents. Multiple chemical, botanical, and "alternative" repellent products are marketed to consumers. We sought to determine which products available in the United States provide reliable and prolonged complete protection from mosquito bites.

Methods We conducted studies involving 15 volunteers to test the relative efficacy of seven botanical insect repellents; four products containing *N,N*-diethyl-*m*-toluamide, now called *N,N*-diethyl-3-methylbenzamide (DEET); a repellent containing IR3535 (ethyl butylacetylaminopropionate); three repellent-impregnated wristbands; and a moisturizer that is commonly claimed to have repellent effects. These products were tested in a controlled laboratory environment in which the species of the mosquitoes, their age, their degree of hunger, the humidity, the temperature, and the light–dark cycle were all kept constant.

Results DEET-based products provided complete protection for the longest duration. Higher concentrations of DEET provided longer-lasting protection. A formulation containing 23.8 percent DEET had a mean complete-protection time of 301.5 minutes. A soybean-oil–based repellent protected against mosquito bites for an average of 94.6 minutes. The IR3535-based repellent protected for an average of 22.9 minutes. All other botanical repellents we tested provided protection for a mean duration of less than 20 minutes. Repellent-impregnated wristbands offered no protection.

Conclusions Currently available non-DEET repellents do not provide protection for durations similar to those of DEET-based repellents and cannot be relied on to provide prolonged protection in environments where mosquito-borne diseases are a substantial threat.

exercise two

Below is a press release from the U.S. Centers for Disease Control about teen smoking. Rewrite and tighten it to follow news style. Keep the story to about 400 words or less. Deadline: 30 minutes.

A new report by the Centers for Disease Control and Prevention (CDC) reveals that although one in four U.S. high school students still smokes cigarettes, rates among this group have been declining since 1997. These findings are from the Youth Risk Behavior Survey (YRBS), part of CDC's Youth Risk Behavior Surveillance System, which is a school-based survey that collects data from students in grades 9-12 nationwide.

According to the report, 28.5 percent of high school students in the United States currently smoke, down from 36.4 percent in 1997. Current smoking is defined as having smoked on one or more of the 30 days preceding the survey. Lifetime use also has declined: In 1999, CDC reported that 70.4 percent of high school students had tried cigarette smoking during their lives. By 2001, that number had fallen to 63.9 percent. The report concludes that if this pattern continues, the United States could achieve the 2010 national health objective of reducing current smoking rates among high school students to 16 percent or less.

"It is encouraging to see more and more teens making the right choice about smoking," said David Fleming, M.D., Acting Director, Centers for Disease Control and Prevention. "We hope this trend continues because it would mean fewer people suffering and dying from smoking-related illnesses.

The data from this report are consistent with other national surveys that suggest the dramatic increase in cigarette smoking rates among high school students during the early to mid-1990s is now being reversed. Factors that might have contributed to the decline in cigarette use include a 70 percent increase in the retail price of cigarettes between December 1997 and May 2001, increases in school-based efforts to prevent tobacco use, and increases in youth exposure to both state and national mass media smoking prevention campaigns.

"While we have made some undeniable progress in reducing the teen smoking rates, now is not the time to rest upon our laurels" warned Rosemarie Henson, M.P.H, M.S.W., di-

rector of CDC's smoking and health program. "Since cigarette prices may not continue to increase, a greater emphasis will need to be put on the school-based efforts and media campaigns that have proven effective as part of comprehensive tobacco control programs so that we can help the next generation of children to remain smoke-free."

Other findings from the study include:

- Current frequent smoking, defined as smoking on at least 20 of the 30 days preceding the survey, decreased from 16.8 percent in 1999 to 13.8 percent in 2001.

- In 2001, as in previous years, white and Hispanic students were significantly more likely than black students to report current smoking.

exercise three

What follows is a press release from the U.S. Centers for Disease Control and Prevention. Rewrite the release in news style and tighten it to about 400 words. Use the Internet to check any terms you don't know. Deadline: 45 minutes.

Centers for Disease Control (CDC), state and local health departments, and the United States Department of Agriculture (USDA) Food Safety and Inspection Service (FSIS) have been investigating an outbreak of listeriosis primarily affecting persons in the northeastern United States. Thus far, 53 ill persons infected with the outbreak strain of *Listeria* have been identified since mid-July; most were hospitalized, eight have died, and three pregnant women have had miscarriages or stillbirths. Epidemiologic data indicate that precooked, sliceable turkey deli meat is the cause of this outbreak.

As part of the ongoing outbreak investigation, USDA-FSIS has been investigating turkey processing plants. *Listeria* bacteria have been found in turkey products and environmental samples from two plants. USDA-FSIS laboratories performed DNA fingerprinting on these bacteria. Comparison of strains was conducted through PulseNet, a network of public health and regulatory laboratories coordinated by

CDC that perform DNA fingerprinting of bacteria and electronically share results.

From Pilgrim's Pride Corporation, located in Franconia, Pennsylvania, two ready-to-eat turkey products and 25 environmental samples tested positive for *Listeria*. The turkey products had strains of *Listeria* different from the outbreak strain. Of the 25 environmental *Listeria* strains fingerprinted, two were indistinguishable from the strain of patients in the current outbreak and several were indistinguishable from strains found in the turkey products. On October 12, the plant voluntarily shut down operations and issued a recall of approximately 27 million pounds of fresh and frozen ready-to-eat turkey and chicken products produced since May 1, 2002. The plant resumed operations on November 13, 2002.

From Jack Lambersky Poultry Company, located in Camden, New Jersey, some ready-to-eat poultry products were contaminated with a strain of *Listeria* that is indistinguishable from that of the outbreak patients. In addition, one environmental sample from the plant tested positive for a strain of *Listeria* different from the outbreak strain. On November 2, the plant voluntarily suspended operations and recalled approximately 200,000 pounds of fresh and frozen ready-to-eat poultry products. The plant subsequently resumed operations on November 14, 2002. On November 20, the plant voluntarily expanded the recall after an additional poultry product tested positive for *Listeria* monocytogenes; DNA fingerprinting of this strain is underway. In addition, approximately 4.2 million pounds of fresh and frozen, ready-to-eat poultry products produced between May 29 and November 2 were recalled.

Turkey meat products included in these recalls should not be eaten. Information on specific products and brands covered by the recalls is available at

http://www.fsis.usda.gov/OA/recalls/prelease/
pr090-2002.htm
http://www.fsis.usda.gov/OA/recalls/prelease/
pr098-2002.htm
http://www.fsis.usda.gov/oa/recalls/prelease/
pr098-2002exp_products.htm.

On November 18, USDA released a draft administrative directive outlining additional measures to be taken by USDA inspectors to ensure that establishments producing ready-to-eat meat and poultry products are taking the necessary steps to prevent contamination with *Listeria* monocytogenes. Information about the draft directive can be found at http://www.usda.gov/news/releases/2002/11/0478.htm.

Listeriosis is a serious foodborne disease that can be life-threatening to certain individuals, including the elderly or those with weakened immune systems. It can also cause miscarriages and stillbirths in pregnant women. The affected patients live in 9 states: Pennsylvania (15 cases), New York (12 cases in New York City, 9 in other locations), New Jersey (5 cases), Delaware (4 cases), Maryland (2 cases), Connecticut (1 case), Michigan (1 case), Massachusetts (3 cases), and Illinois (1 case). Thirty-two patients were male and 21 were female. Sixteen patients were age 65 or above, 17 patients were age 1 to 64 years and had an immunocompromising medical condition, eight others were pregnant, and four were neonates; seven patients were age 1 to 64 years and were not pregnant or known to have an immunocompromising condition. No medical information was available for one patient. Of the eight patients who died, seven had immunocompromising conditions (three of these patients were also age 65 or older), and one was a neonate. The culture date

for the most recent patient was October 26. In addition to the patients whose illnesses have been confirmed as part of the outbreak, CDC and state and local health departments have learned about other cases of *Listeria* infection in the same region during the outbreak time period. DNA fingerprinting has shown that strains from 98 patients in these same states are different from the outbreak strain and 24 of these patients have died; these illnesses are part of the "background" of sporadic *Listeria* infections and are likely due to a variety of different foods. In addition, testing of strains from several additional persons is ongoing; some of these may be identified as the outbreak strain. Because pregnant women, older adults, and people with weakened immune systems are at higher risk for listeriosis, we recommend the following measures for those persons:

- Do not eat hot dogs and luncheon meats, unless they are reheated until steaming hot.
- Avoid cross-contaminating other foods, utensils, and food preparation surfaces with fluid from hot dog packages, and wash hands after handling hot dogs.
- Do not eat soft cheeses such as Feta, Brie and Camembert cheeses, blue-veined cheeses, and Mexican-style cheeses such as "queso blanco fresco." Cheeses that may be eaten include hard cheeses; semi-soft cheeses such as mozzarella; pasteurized processed cheeses such as slices and spreads; cream cheese; and cottage cheese.
- Do not eat refrigerated pâtés or meat spreads. Canned or shelf-stable pâtés and meat spreads may be eaten.
- Do not eat refrigerated smoked seafood, unless it is contained in a cooked dish, such as a casserole. Refrigerated smoked seafood, such as salmon, trout, whitefish, cod, tuna or mackerel, is most often labeled as "nova-style," "lox," "kippered," "smoked," or "jerky." The fish is found in the refrigerator section or sold at deli counters of grocery stores and delicatessens. Canned or shelf-stable smoked seafood may be eaten.
- Do not drink raw (unpasteurized) milk or eat foods that contain unpasteurized milk.

About 2,500 cases of listeriosis occur each year in the United States. The initial symptoms are often fever, muscle aches, and sometimes gastrointestinal symptoms such as nausea or diarrhea. The illness may be mild and ill persons sometimes describe their illness as flu-like. If infection spreads to the nervous system, symptoms such as headache, stiff neck, confusion, loss of balance, or convulsions can occur. Most cases of listeriosis and most deaths occur in adults with weakened immune systems, the elderly, pregnant women, and newborns. However, infections can occur occasionally in otherwise healthy persons. Infections during pregnancy can lead to miscarriages, stillbirths, and infection of newborn infants. Previous outbreaks of listeriosis have been linked to a variety of foods especially processed meats (such as hot dogs, deli meats, and paté) and dairy products made from unpasteurized milk.

The risk of an individual person developing *Listeria* infection after consumption of a conta-minated product is very small. If you have eaten a contaminated product and do not have any symptoms, we do not recommend that you have any tests or treatment, even if you are in a high risk group. However, if you are in a high risk group, have eaten the contaminated product, and within a month become ill with fever or signs of serious illness, you should contact your health care provider and inform him or her about this exposure.

If you have questions about *Listeria*, you can call your local or state health department, your physician, or visit the CDC Web site at http://www. cdc.gov/ncidod/dbmd/diseaseinfo/ listeriosis_g.htm or visit the USDA Web site at http://www.usda.gov/ news/releases/2001/01/0020.htm.

exercise four

Rewrite the following press release from the Centers for Disease Control and Prevention in news style. Keep the story to about 400 words. Deadline: 45 minutes.

Despite continued declines among African Americans and women of all races, overall rates of primary and secondary syphilis have increased slightly for the first time in more than a decade, according to a new report from the Centers for Disease Control and Prevention (CDC). The report, published in the November 1 issue of CDC's *Morbidity and Mortality Weekly Report,* found that cases of primary and secondary syphilis in the United States rose by 2 percent between 2000 and 2001 (5,979 cases in 2000 to 6,103 cases in 2001). The overall syphilis rate in the United States increased from 2.1 per 100,000 people to 2.2 per 100,000 people, the first such increase since 1990.

The report, by CDC epidemiologist Dr. James Heffelfinger, attributed the slight increase to syphilis diagnoses among men. Syphilis rates among U.S. men rose by 15.4 percent between 2000 and 2001, an increase that coincided with outbreaks among gay and bisexual men in several U.S. cities.

These increases contrast with significant and sustained progress in syphilis elimination in populations and areas where syphilis rates are high-est—among African Americans and individuals living in the South. Syphilis cases among African Americans declined by 9.9 percent between 2000 and 2001 (3.5 percent and 18.1 percent among African-American men and women, respectively). Additionally, although the South continues to have the largest proportion of syphilis cases (56 percent of total U.S. cases), there was an 8 percent decline in syphilis rates in this region. Syphilis cases among women overall declined by 19.5 percent. These declines were consistent with those noted every year since CDC began syphilis elimination efforts in 1998, targeting groups and regions at highest risk.

"These data show that a careful, concerted effort to eliminate this disease can work. Ultimately, our success will depend on the continued and careful targeting of our prevention resources to those areas and populations most affected by syphilis, including gay and bisexual men," said Dr. Ronald O. Valdiserri, deputy director of CDC's HIV, STD and TB prevention programs.

NEW CHALLENGES

Centers for Disease Control (CDC) officials said that increases in syphilis among gay and bisexual men of all races pose new challenges to U.S. efforts to eliminate the disease. Syphilis cases among white and Latino men increased by 63 percent and 50 percent, respectively, from 2000 to 2001. Additionally, although African-American men were the only men in any racial or ethnic group to experience a decline, the 3.5 percent decline among African-American men represents a significant slowing in the large decline reported last year (15 percent decline from 1999 to 2000).

The report indicates that the increases seen among men are associated with recent syphilis outbreaks among gay and bisexual men of all races and highlights outbreaks reported in Chicago, Los Angeles, New York City, San Francisco, Seattle and Miami.

Health officials said that because the risk behaviors for syphilis and HIV are similar, and because syphilis lesions increase risk of HIV transmission between two and five times, outbreaks among gay and bisexual men could also signal a potential increase in HIV transmission.

"Our challenge—and the challenge for gay and bisexual communities across America—is to underscore the connections between syphilis and HIV, and to renew the kind of commitment these communities brought to HIV prevention in the early years of the epidemic," Valdiserri said.

CDC is actively investigating the factors that have made some gay and bisexual men particularly vulnerable to syphilis, working with community organizations and local health departments on research and health interventions to understand current trends and avoid future outbreaks. CDC also is working to improve national STD surveillance to include information on risk behavior, including same-gender partners.

In recent years, CDC has dispatched rapid response teams to help local health departments control outbreaks; helped develop Internet interventions to alert men to the dangers of syphilis transmission and the need for testing; funded community health campaigns; intensified HIV prevention efforts; and used mobile vans and other innovative strategies to make syphilis testing available in predominantly gay neighborhoods, bathhouses, HIV clinics and community health centers.

LOCAL DATA

The CDC report also highlighted syphilis trends among counties across the United States. The report found that half of the nation's syphilis cases were concentrated in 20 counties and one independent city. Overall, 80 percent of all U.S. counties did not report a single case of primary or secondary syphilis in 2001. Despite the increase in syphilis cases among gay and bisexual men, CDC officials said that the national goal of eliminating syphilis by 2005 (defined as 90 percent of counties syphilis-free) remained in effect.

"We cannot and should not accept a rise in syphilis cases in any population as the 'way things are,'" said Valdiserri. "We're beating this disease in the communities most disproportionately affected by syphilis, and we have to continue our efforts to achieve and maintain the elimination of this disease."

Real REPORTER: Daniel Q. Haney

It's a reporter's job to make complex information understandable. On Daniel Q. Haney's beat, that's not easy. Haney is the medical editor of The Associated Press. Not only does he oversee coverage of the medical beat for the world's largest news organization, he also writes plenty of his own stories. Chronicling the latest advances in medical research and technology on a tight deadline requires superb journalistic skills. It also requires a broad knowledge of the subject matter—knowledge Haney has acquired during more than 20 years of medical writing.

Haney brought all his skills to bear while covering a recent medical conference in Atlanta. "At these conferences there are typically thousands of scientific presentations going on," Haney says. "The hard part is finding a story to write every day, because most of it is highly technical and tedious, of interest only to other researchers."

Haney learned of a news briefing about a new advance in angioplasty, a technique for opening clogged arteries. He knew the research was important—heart disease is the single largest cause of death worldwide. And while angioplasty has been around for decades, the procedure had been plagued by problems. A new advance might hold promise for tens of thousands of heart patients.

Haney did some background research on angioplasty, then attended the briefing. Although held for journalists, most of those attending work for the medical trade press, so it was conducted in the language of doctors, not ordinary people. Plenty of technical medical jargon was thrown around, but Haney, armed with the background research he had done and knowledge culled from articles he'd previously written on the subject, understood the lingo. "I knew the history of this endeavor. I knew what problems there had been over the years, and I was very aware of why this was a big deal."

Afterward, Haney had to move quickly. Each day around lunchtime, the AP sends out the news digest to its subscribers nationwide. The digest lists the top stories of the day from around the world, and describes how the AP plans to cover them. The AP news digest is very influential, since editors and broadcast news producers use it to help plan their own coverage. Putting a story on the news digest almost guarantees it will be carried by hundreds of newspapers and broadcast outlets. In order to get his story noticed on the AP's national news wire digest, Haney sent a one-line description of the story—similar to a lead—to the AP's national editing desk. The AP editors could then put the description, called a digest line, onto the national news digest.

After sending his digest line, Haney could have taken several hours to write his story. But just as newspapers compete to get the story first, the AP competes with smaller wire services. Haney likes to beat the competition by getting his articles out on the wire first. "Over the years I've found that it's better not to send stories out late in the day. There's a lot of competition at newspaper wire desks. All the copy seems to arrive in the late afternoon. If you can beat that traffic jam your stories have a lot better chance of getting in the paper. I like to see my stories get on the wire before 3 p.m., which means they have to be written, edited and sent out long before my competitors' stories are done. I can often beat them by several hours, and that guarantees that my story will get into print."

With the angioplasty story, Haney gave himself about an hour to write. One challenge, he says, "was to go beyond just the nitty gritty facts . . . and to convey how very important this new method was, to step back from the details and try to give readers the big picture." Indeed, Haney says one of the most difficult tasks a science or medical reporter faces is making the reader understand why something is significant. "Anyone can write a story with a bunch of statistics," he says. "But putting it into perspective, saying why it's important and how it affects your health decisions—that's the hard part. That kind of perspective has to be in every story."

The other big challenge of a beat like Haney's is taking highly complex information and making it clear to average reader. He has his own technique for achieving this. "I try to put myself in the position of a reader who is intelligent but not highly educated—maybe someone with a high school degree," he says. "I try to read the story from their point of view, and think to myself whether all the words would be understandable. I try to remove all technical jargon and put it into plain English."

That even applies to seemingly straightforward words like "trial," Haney says, which in medicine refers to a research study. "I even avoid words like that. Some people may understand them but others may think it's what happens in a courtroom." While student journalists will probably find this kind of simplification takes practice, Haney says, "It was easy for me from the beginning, because I didn't know what these words meant myself," Haney says.

"It was easy to put myself in the position of someone who was not trained in medicine or science. I was always very conscious of the need to translate things."

Haney, a New England native, earned his bachelor's degree in journalism from Boston University. While in college he worked summers in the AP's bureau in Portland, Maine, then transferred to the Boston bureau after graduation. During the 1970s he covered the battles over school integration and busing in Boston. Then, in 1978, the Boston bureau's science writer transferred to Washington. "The week he left, the news editor threw the 'New England Journal of Medicine' down on my desk and said, 'See if there's anything in there,' " Haney recalls. "I'd never looked at a medical journal in my life, but I looked through it, found something I thought I could understand, and wrote a story."

The story was sent out on the AP's national wire, and soon Haney was flipping through the pages of the prestigious medical journal every week, looking for research that might be of interest to a wide readership. Haney became a full-time medical writer in the early 1980s, and in 1996 was appointed medical editor.

Haney says when he writes on deadline, he constructs a mental outline of the story. "I know the major points in my head. I go over all the material, the key elements. In the end it's all a matter of concentration, of not being distracted by the noise and people around you. Just immerse yourself in that one small subject for an hour and don't think of anything else."

And the angioplasty story? Haney's article went out on the national wire and was carried by hundreds of newspapers. He had beaten the competition—again. Below is Haney's story as it appeared on the AP wire:

ATLANTA—A new approach to keeping heart arteries flowing smoothly after angioplasty shows astonishing success in early testing, apparently solving a major shortcoming of this common procedure.

Doctors on Sunday released the longest follow-up with the new technique—the drug-coated stent. In testing on 43 patients over two years, they found it to be 100 percent effective, an accomplishment almost unheard of in medicine.

More than 1 million Americans undergo angioplasty annually, and the new approach is likely to be used on most of them if these promising early results hold up in further testing. They could be on the market as early as next year.

"This is a very hot topic, potentially revolutionary in the treatment of coronary artery disease," said Dr. Spencer King III of Emory University.

During angioplasty, doctors fish tiny balloons through clogged heart arteries, then inflate them briefly to open up blood flow. Frequently, though, the arteries squeeze shut again. In recent years, doctors have often left behind tiny wire coils, called stents, to prop the arteries open.

However, about one-quarter of the time, the reopened artery closes off, a condition called restenosis. It usually occurs when fast-growth scar-like tissue fills the artery, and it must be fixed with a repeat angioplasty or a coronary bypass.

The solution to this dilemma appears to be a new kind of stent that is coated with medicines that gradually ooze into the artery. The drugs keep cells from growing.

The first hint of their potential was made public last September at a European heart conference, and more data were released Sunday at a meeting of the American College of Cardiology in Atlanta.

At least eight different varieties—coated with different growth-inhibiting medicines—are now in testing, and many more are under development. The first was Cordis Corp.'s stent coated with the immune-suppressing drug rapamycin, tested on patients in Brazil and the Netherlands.

Dr. J. Eduardo Sousa of the Dante Pazzanese Institute of Cardiology in São Paulo presented two years of follow-up with those 43 initial patients. While three of them have needed heart procedures for worsening disease in other parts of their hearts, all of the areas treated with the Cordis stents are flowing freely.

Sousa projected an X-ray of one of the patient's hearts, showing a wide, obstruction-free artery. "No lesion. No problem," he said. "The artery is completely open after two years' follow-up."

Dr. Jean Fajadet of Thoraxcenter in Rotterdam gave results with the same stent after seven months in 238 patients. Again, not a single stent clogged up, compared with restenosis in 26 percent of those getting ordinary stents.

Dr. Sidney Smith, chief medical officer of the American Heart Association, cautioned that large, careful studies must be finished comparing the new stents with the ordinary kind.

Nevertheless, he said, "these are very impressive and very encouraging results. When you see zero restenosis at one year, it's a breakthrough. It's almost too good to believe when you see zero." Especially encouraging, Smith said, is the fact they seem to work in unusually small arteries and in those of diabetic patients. Both are very prone to reclogging.

Dr. Greg Stone of Lenox Hill Hospital in New York City said the first of these stents could be available in 2003. Results of at least three large studies, necessary to win Food and Drug Administration approval, are expected on rival products within the next year.

Manufacturers have not said how much they will cost, but Stone said the price is likely to be about double that of ordinary stents, which sell for around $1,400 apiece.

King said the cost might limit their use, since doctors often install several stents during an angioplasty.

Reprinted with permission of The Associated Press.

INTERNET EXERCISES

Many federal agencies and scientific journals have Web sites that includes press releases on recent scientific research. These releases can be used as the basis for newswriting exercises.

The New England Journal of Medicine: **http://www.nejm.org**

The Journal of the American Medical Association: **http://www.jama.com**

The National Science Foundation: **http://www.nsf.gov**

The Centers for Disease Control: **http://www.cdc.gov**

The National Institutes of Health: **http://www.nih.gov**

The National Institute of Child Health and Human Development: **http://www.nichd.nih.gov**

BEYOND THE CLASSROOM

If you attend a large university where scientific research is done, look into what kinds of studies are being conducted on campus. If there's a study you think might be interesting to a general audience, see if you can interview one of the researchers and write a story.

13

Features

So far in this book you've been learning to write in a hard-news format. The inverted pyramid, the five W's and the H, leads of 35 words or less—these are all elements of what editors sometimes call "straight" newswriting. It's a tried-and-true formula that has served reporters well for many years.

But there is another method. For a variety of reasons, reporters sometimes prefer to use a more feature-oriented approach to their articles. This style, which is similar in many ways to magazine writing, frees reporters to tell their stories in a more leisurely, creative way. For certain types of stories, under certain circumstances, a feature-oriented approach is undoubtedly the best way to go.

Perhaps the most important difference between straight hard-news stories and feature articles is in the lead. As we've said, the hard-news format demands that the reporter get the main point of the story into the very first paragraph. But feature-oriented leads, often called delayed leads, have no such requirement. In a delayed lead, the reporter has the luxury of letting his story unfold more slowly, over the course of two or three paragraphs.

For example, the reporter might spend the first few paragraphs of his story relating an anecdote that's relevant to the subject (feature leads are also sometimes called anecdotal leads). Or he might use the first few paragraphs to describe a place or person, or set a scene. Here are the first two paragraphs of a feature story about college students who also work odd jobs:

> *It was Tuesday afternoon at Burger World, and Jane Krason was working the 3-to-11 shift at the cash register, ringing up cheeseburgers, fries and shakes. She'd just come from four hours of classes at Centerville State College.*
>
> *Later that night, at the end of her shift, she would drive home and spend another three hours cracking the books, finally getting to sleep at around 3 a.m. Just another average day for Krason, a full-time student who also just happens to work 35 hours a week.*

As you can see, this represents a dramatic departure from a straight hard-news lead. The writer doesn't even attempt to get the five W's and the H into the first paragraph. Instead, he uses the first two paragraphs to *begin* to tell a story about Jane Krason. Notice we use the phrase "tell a story." That's important—storytelling is what feature writing is all about. Straight hard-newswriting turns traditional storytelling on its head by putting the most important information right at the start of the story. Feature writing is an attempt to tell stories in a more traditional, linear way.

But there are limits. Even a feature article must eventually get to the point. Feature articles do this in what's called a "nut graph." A nut graph is essentially the "lead" of the feature story. It explains to the reader what the story is about, what the main point is. But instead of being the story's first paragraph, the nut graph comes after the first few paragraphs of the delayed lead. Here again is the story about Jane Krason, this time with the nut graph added:

> *It was Tuesday afternoon at Burger World, and Jane Krason was working the 3-to-11 shift at the cash register, ringing up cheeseburgers, fries and shakes. She'd just come from four hours of classes at Centerville State College.*
>
> *Later that night, at the end of her shift, she would drive home and spend another three hours cracking the books, finally getting to sleep at around 3 a.m. Just another average day for Krason, a full-time student who also just happens to work 35 hours a week.*
>
> *Krason, 19, is one of thousands of Centerville State College students who work outside jobs in addition to taking classes. With financial aid drying up nationwide, more and more students say they must work to make ends meet.*
>
> *But many students, particularly those who work 30 hours a week or more, say the workload is bound to take a toll, especially on their grades.*

The first two graphs are the delayed lead. They begin to tell the story of Jane Krason. The next two graphs are the nut graphs (there can be more than one) that explain to the reader what the story is all about, that is, the problems of college students who work long hours at outside jobs.

Even with a feature approach, readers still want to get to the point of the story fairly quickly. Generally, you should reach the nut graph within the first three or four paragraphs of your article.

As noted earlier, a feature-oriented approach is best for certain types of stories. What types of stories are not suitable for this approach? Generally, big, breaking hard-news stories, which should be written with a hard-news lead. Wars, natural disasters, plane crashes, important elections or political developments, verdicts in big court cases, and any sort of calamity that involves loss of human life—these should usually be written with a straight lead. To see why, try putting a feature lead on say, a story about the president declaring war:

The president wore a navy blue suit and maroon tie. He fidgeted with his cufflinks but then appeared confident as he stepped in front of a phalanx of TV cameras. Outside it was cloudy, an ominous foreshadowing of what was to come.

"I am announcing today," he said, clearing his throat, "that the United States has begun invading Iraq in an effort to end that country's support for worldwide terrorism."

Pretty silly, right? No right-minded reporter would ever put that kind of a lead on a story of such import. Readers don't care about the color of the president's tie or the fact that he fidgeted. They want the news—the fact that the U.S. is invading Iraq—fast.

But feature leads can be used very effectively on events of lesser importance, ones that aren't necessary so closely tied to a breaking news event. For instance, if your city elects a new mayor, that's probably a hard-news-lead story. But if you write a profile of the new mayor, showing what she's like at home with her husband and kids, that's a story that cries out for a feature lead. In other words, stories that have less of a hard-news "edge" to them are often appropriate for a feature approach.

Feature leads aren't just for "soft" news, however. Breaking news events that aren't necessarily of earth-shaking importance and that occur relatively early in the news day can also sometimes be written with a feature approach. Indeed, newspapers have increasingly been using feature leads in recent years, even on some hard-news stories. One reason is the rise of television, 24-hour cable news and the Internet. Events that occur relatively early in the day will probably be on the evening news, and readers will know all about them by the time they pick up their paper the next morning. So reporters often take a feature-oriented approach to these types of stories.

Feature leads are also used in what are known as sidebars. Sidebars are articles that accompany the main news article about an event, but that focus on one particular aspect of that event. For instance, if you're covering the mayoral election, you'll have a hard-news story that includes the results of the balloting, the statements by the candidates and a summary of the issues involved in the race. But, since a mayoral election is such an important event, your newspaper might also include a sidebar focusing on the election-night scene at the candidates' campaign headquarters or interviews with local residents, getting their reactions to the campaign.

At the end of this chapter you'll read a sidebar written by reporter Vanessa Ho, a reporter for the Seattle Post-Intelligencer. When a Seattle-bound plane crashed into the ocean, Ho's paper carried a straight hard-news account of the tragedy. But Ho's assignment was to write specifically about the scene at the airport, where relatives of those on the doomed flight were waiting for their loved ones to arrive. As you'll see, Ho took a feature-oriented approach to her story.

The lead isn't the only thing different about a feature story. The body of such a story generally includes more quotes, color and description than hard-news stories. Indeed, hard-news stories generally don't spend much time describing the people who are being quoted or interviewed in them. If you're writing a story about what sparked a fire that destroyed a building, readers aren't interested in a detailed description of the fire marshal you interviewed. They want to know the cause of the fire. But in a feature story where you profile the fire marshal, you most definitely must include a physical description of him. Without that, the story would be incomplete and unsatisfying for readers.

One good way to think about feature writing is to remember your five senses—sight, hearing, smell, touch and taste. Feature stories should convey to a reader what a person, place or thing looks like, sounds like, and so on. This can be done in hard-news stories as well, but it's an absolute necessity in a well-written feature.

Beginning reporters often have the mistaken impression that reporters writing feature articles don't have deadlines. Although it's true that on certain types of longer feature stories, reporters are given more time than they would be on a deadline news story, more often than not, feature articles have to be banged out just as quickly as hard-news stories.

QUICK TIPS

- Feature leads consist of several opening paragraphs, usually no more than three, that lead the reader into the story through the use of description or anecdote, or by setting a scene.

- Once that description or anecdote has been established, the nut graph comes next. The nut graph explains what the story is about. It's the *lead* of your feature article.

- Hard-news leads are generally used for very important breaking news events. Feature leads can be for events of lesser importance, for events that happen early in the news day, for stories that are less time-sensitive than breaking news, and on sidebars that accompany the main news story about a event.

exercise one

This exercise was in Chapter 6, "Stormy Weather and Natural Disasters." In that chapter you were asked to write the article as a hard-news story. This time, assume that you are writing a sidebar that should be done in a more feature-oriented style. Deadline: 40 minutes.

Hurricane Bonnie has hit Barco, a small coastal town in North Carolina. Write a story based on your notes taken at the scene. Deadline: 30 minutes.

The storm is bearing down on the Carolina coast and the entire town has been evacuated. High winds have knocked out power to the town and a storm surge has flooded roads everywhere. Driving through the streets that are still passable, there are trees flattened and sparks flying from downed power lines. The winds ripped the roof off St. Mary's Hospital and dozens of patients had to be evacuated to St. Marks, the town's other main hospital. Cops and civil defense people are about the only people on the streets, except for 83-year-old Jake Wilson, who's standing on the porch of his tiny bungalow. Wilson is a widower who has decided to sit out the storm. He says: "I've seen these storms come and go for years and I've always survived. I didn't move then, I ain't moving now." The police say that one person, a 12-year-old child, was killed when a tree fell on her house. Three other people have been injured in the storm so far. The police don't have any names yet.

exercise two

This exercise was in Chapter 9, "Sports." In that chapter you were asked to write the article as a straight sports story. This time, write the story in a more feature-oriented style, using a delayed lead. Deadline: 45 minutes.

You're covering a high school football game between the George School and visiting Perkiomen High. Here are your notes:

George School took an early 7-0 lead on a Rob Waters run. Perkiomen came back with a touchdown in each of the first three quarters, including a two-point conversion in the second quarter on an option play caught by Sean Singletary, nephew of former Chicago Bears great Mike Singletary. Larry Andrews' 81-yard TD run gave Perkiomen School a 22-7 lead in the third quarter. George School bounced back in the fourth, when Waters rushed for another touchdown. He ended the day with 184 yards rushing. But Perkiomen sealed the win with a safety in the fourth period. After the game, George School quarterback Jon Compitello says, "I wish we could have won, but what it all comes down to is the experience. It's about having fun and the brothership." George School coach John Gleeson says, "These kids played their hearts out. They gave everything they could, especially the seniors." George School ends the year 4-4, losing its last three games after winning four in a row at one point. The game is the last one to be played together by George School senior split ends Ben Fisher and Ryan Mellon. The two Doylestown residents have been best friends since first grade. They have been attending school together ever since they can remember. But they'll be going to different colleges next fall. "It's real tough," Mellon says after the game. "It's bittersweet. You always want to win your last game, but we battled the whole way. That's the way to go out. It still hasn't sunk it yet that my high school football career is over." Fisher adds, "The four years I put into this program, all the pain, the sweat, the blood, I wouldn't trade it for anything. I look at these 30 guys as my second family. It really hurts to lose the last one. It's been great for the team to have the two split ends as best friends, but next year, we'll be going to different schools, so that'll be different." Final score: Perkiomen 24, George School 14.

exercise three

Write a story based on the following information. Deadline: 45 minutes.

The fire department today was called to a house where something crashed through the roof. Your source in the department gives you the name of the people living there: Eileen and Alphonse Danowski. You call, and get Eileen on the phone. She tells you she and her husband live in a two-bedroom home, and are both 69. She says that a chunk of what looked like brown ice crashed through her roof and landed on her kitchen floor just three feet away from her while she was cooking. The ice chunk, about the size of a bowling ball, ripped an 8-inch-by-12-inch hole in their roof and ceiling and broke plates in the kitchen cabinets. "All of a sudden it was like an explosion. It was all over the floor. I backed away from it, saw there wasn't a fire, then said, 'I'm getting out of here,'" she says. Eileen got her husband and they called the fire department, who examined the chunk and told the Danowskis it was a chunk of frozen human waste dropped from a jet's latrine in the skies overhead. Fire officials told Mrs. Danowski that if the chunk had hit her, it could have killed her.

"I've heard of manna from heaven, but this wasn't the right kind of manna," Eileen tells you. "Someone pushed the wrong button or something. It was gross, believe me. We had to leave it there all day, and it smelled," she adds. "The police photographer had to come, and the insurance guy had to come out. He thought we were kidding."

Joan Brown, the spokeswoman for the regional office of the Federal Aviation Administration, tells you the incident is "completely under investigation." She says bathroom waste sometimes seeps to the outside hull of airliners, then it freezes and drops to the ground.

exercise four

Write a story based on the following information. Deadline: one hour.

A police source tells you a homeless man was found dead on the plaza in front of City Hall, a very busy area in the heart of the city's downtown. He says the man had been dead about four hours when someone finally took a look at him. The man has been identified as Joseph Bulens, 49. You call the coroner, who says Bulens died of natural causes.

Acting on a hunch, you call Ken Smith, director of the Shelter for Homeless Veterans, which is near City Hall. Smith says Bulens was often at the shelter. Smith says Bulens joined the Air Force as a young man but when his 16-year-old sister died he returned home to work in a factory to help support his family. Bulens got married but the marriage went sour and he started drinking and he ended up on the street. "Joe Bulens would give you the shirt off his back. Even when he was inebriated, he was a pleasant guy. But he had a difficult time with his pain. He medicated himself with booze."

You head to the spot where Bulens was found. You see a man standing there. He identifies himself as David Solomon, and says he was the one who discovered Bulens. Solomon says he was working in his ninth-floor City Hall office at about 10 a.m. when he saw Bulens splayed out on the sidewalk. Solomon said he was worried at first, but then saw a well-dressed man sitting on a bench just 10 feet away. "I thought, 'He must just be asleep or that guy would do something,' " Solomon tells you.

But when Solomon looked out his window again 45 minutes later, Bulens was still lying there and the well-dressed man was gone. Solomon went to check Bulens out. "His hands had no color, they were pale. His face was purplish pink. He looked like he'd been there for a while."

Solomon said he tried to get help from three passersby, but no one would stop. Finally he hailed a police car. Firefighters were called, and they covered the body with a sheet. Solomon is angry. "This shows that as long as you have a roof over your head, who gives a damn about the other guy," he says.

exercise five

Write a story based on the following information. Deadline: one hour.

Members of the Titanic Historical Society are gathering in town this week to commemorate the anniversary of the sinking of the great ship. You've been assigned to write a feature story on the anniversary. You interview historian Donald Lynch, who has written about the Titanic. He tells you the ship had Turkish baths, a gym, a French sidewalk cafe. Its passenger list reads like a who's who of the day.

Lynch says when the Titanic hit the iceberg its hull was ripped open and the ship began to list. Women and children were put on lifeboats, but there wasn't enough room for everyone. Some people couldn't believe the ship would sink and refused to leave. Lynch tells you about one of the Titanic survivors he interviewed, Nellie Becker. Becker told Lynch she awoke at 11:40 p.m. because the hum of the ship's engines had stopped. She left her cabin to ask a steward if something was wrong. He said nothing was wrong. Becker went back to bed but was worried and couldn't sleep. She got up again and found another steward, who told her, "Go back to your cabin, get your lifebelts and your children and get up on deck."

"Do we have time to dress?" she asked him. "No madam," he said. "You have time for nothing." Becker and her children got onto a lifeboat. She died years later. Her grandchildren are at the Historical Society meeting this week.

Lynch also interviewed Mrs. Becker's daughter, Ruth, who was 12 at the time of the sinking. She got separated from her mother and was forced to find another lifeboat. She offered blankets to crewmen, bandaged a man's finger and helped a woman find her baby after they were picked up by a rescue ship. Before she died in 1990—at age 90—Ruth told Lynch the saddest thing she recalled were the scores of women who lined the decks of the rescue ship Carpathia, looking out to sea for lifeboats that might bring their husbands. Then, the Carpathia started its engines to leave. "That's when they knew they were widows," Ruth told him.

Lynch also tell you about examples of courage during the sinking. Ida Straus, wife of Macy's founder Isidor Straus, refused to leave the ship without her husband, who had to stay behind with the men. Both went down with the ship. Also, there was Edwina Troutt, a single woman who was horrified that men couldn't board lifeboats with their wives. She refused to leave the ship until a man carrying an infant came to her and said, "I don't want to be saved, but who will save this baby?" Only then did she take the child and board a lifeboat.

You interview Louise Pope, a Titanic survivor who was 4 at the time. She says interest in the sinking remains strong. She says, "Even now, I go to schools and talk to children, and they're all excited about it. When they see me, it's quite a thing."

Titanic Historical Society President Edward Kamuda tells you, "It's the whole drama of the thing. A ship on its maiden voyage, with high society people onboard, hitting an iceberg on a calm night. It's the impossible tragedy that never should have happened."

Use the Internet to dig up some background information about the Titanic. Combine it with your interviews when you write your story.

Real REPORTER: Vanessa Ho

It was late afternoon at the Seattle Post-Intelligencer when word came in of a huge story—a Seattle-bound passenger jet had crashed off the California coast. Early reports indicated there were no survivors.

The paper's editors knew they had to have a big main news story, or mainbar, that would include all the details of the crash and the search and rescue operation. They also wanted to have a secondary story, or sidebar, on the scene at Seattle's Sea-Tac Airport, where relatives would be waiting for loved ones from the doomed flight.

But the paper's first edition deadline was fast approaching. There was no time to send a reporter (in rush-hour traffic) to Sea-Tac to gather information, then return to the newsroom and write a story. So a team of reporters was dispatched to the airport and veteran reporter Vanessa Ho was assigned to rewrite duty on the story.

A rewrite person remains in the newsroom, taking down information called in from other reporters at the scene of an event, including facts, quotes, color and background. She has the challenging task of taking that hodgepodge of data and fashioning it into a coherent article. More often than not, the rewrite person works on a very tight deadline. "The crash happened around 4:30 p.m. That's pretty late in the day to hear about a big breaking story," Ho recalls. "We sent five people to the airport, and my job was to take all the feeds that were coming in from the reporters. It was really crazy."

As Ho waited for reporters to get to the airport, she worked the phones, trying to gather what information she could from the airline and airport officials. "Probably around 6 or 6:30 I finally started getting stuff from reporters at the scene," Ho says. "It took them a long time to find people to talk to. This was the first time I had done rewrite on a big breaking story, and it was really stressful," she adds. "Part of the problem was, I wasn't there myself at the airport to see what was going on. So I had to interview the reporters who were there about the interviews they had done. You know the material better when you're the reporter on the scene, instead of having to take someone else's notes and turn them into a story."

After taking the reporters' "feeds," Ho had about 90 minutes until deadline to construct a story. She had to decide on what kind of lead to use. "There are times when I know I'm going to use a feature lead, but when I set out to write this story I didn't know what the lead would be. But this was a story about the human impact of the crash. And we already had a hard-news story about the crash." So she wrote a feature lead that described the terrible jolt relatives must have felt as they arrived at the airport and learned of the crash. "What struck me was the enormous grief at the airport," she recalls. "I tried to put myself in the shoes of the people there. There's the shock of thinking you're picking up a loved one coming back from vacation, and instead you have to confront this horrible tragedy."

Ho, who has covered a variety of beats since starting at the Post-Intelligencer in 1994, often considers the timing of a story when deciding whether to use a feature lead. If an event happens early in the day, she knows her readers will probably hear about it on the evening news. In that case, she's more likely to use a feature lead "to try to advance the story," she says. "But if it's something that happens at night, and the first time people will learn about it is in the morning paper, then I'll be more likely to use a straight news lead. With features, I try to emphasize themes and the mood more, and to put a little more personality into the story." The key, she says, "is to always ask yourself, why am I writing this story? What is it someone would want to learn from this story?"

Ho, a California native, majored in English at UCLA, then earned a master's degree in journalism at UC-Berkeley. She worked at Seattle's other big paper, The Seattle Times, for two years before joining the Post-Intelligencer. Here is the sidebar story Ho wrote about the crash.

They were supposed to embrace loved ones stepping off the plane, many of whom would probably be tan and happy after a vacation in Puerto Vallarta, Mexico.

Instead, they rushed into Sea-Tac Airport in tears after learning that Alaska Airlines Flight 261 had crashed into the Pacific Ocean yesterday, about 20 miles off the California coast near Los Angeles.

As a stream of frantic people made their way to Alaska's counter last night, employees escorted them into a private "family room" with counselors and clergy on the second-floor mezzanine.

"I think my sister is on that flight," said one man. Other people came in holding hands and holding back tears.

One young woman, crying hysterically, said her mother is a Seattle-based Alaska Airlines attendant who was on a flight in Mexico yesterday. But she did not know which flight.

"This is probably one of the most tragic days this airline has experienced," said Jack Evans, Alaska Airlines spokesman. "I think we're all in shock, just like everyone else is."

Eighty-three passengers and five crew members had been on board Flight 261. Forty-seven of the passengers had been booked to Seattle, and three crew members were also from Seattle. The two pilots were from Los Angeles.

Alaska employees said last night that 30 of those on board either worked for Horizon Air and its parent company, Alaska Airlines, or were friends or family members.

"Our thoughts and our prayers at this moment are for our passengers and fellow employees and for their families, friends and loved ones. To all I extend my personal and profound sorrow for what has transpired," Alaska Airlines Chief Executive Officer John Kelly said in a statement.

In the private room, a specially trained team of Alaska's employees provided care, support and food and set up a hot line for family members.

Chaplain John Oas said the mood in the room was somber. He said about a dozen family members and a dozen employees and friends whispered in hushed tones and hugged one another.

He said the people were grieving, but still held hope.

"I would say there is always (hope) holding out in the human heart," he said.

Lynnette Arnold and Jeff Peterson, both of Federal Way, were two of many people of faith who arrived to provide support. Arnold said she was at home when she heard the news on TV. She then called Peterson, who attends her church.

"We were just shocked," she said, while waiting by the ticket counter. "The spirit of God came on and said get down to the airport right now."

Capt. Maynard Sargent of the Salvation Army, a King James Bible in hand, also arrived to help. And nine people with the American Red Cross were also providing support.

The crash shook up Alaska's employees, and some attendants cried during their flights into Seattle.

Alaska pilot Scott Borden had flown Flight 261 the day before and was getting ready for a flight to California last night. "It brought it home," he said.

He was thinking of what he would tell his upcoming passengers. "Hopefully I can come up with some comforting words," he said.

A flight attendant who was part of Alaska's critical incident response team was debriefing all crew members who arrived at Sea-Tac. The attendant, who didn't want to be named, knew the crew members, but declined to discuss them.

"We're just making sure the crews are OK," he said, adding that 1,200 of Alaska's 2,000 flight attendants live in Seattle. "We all know everybody."

At Gate C9, where Alaska flight 237 had arrived from Puerta Vallarta, passengers and families sobbed at their brush with fate. A girls' gymnastics team from Auburn was on the plane, and many parents had waited anxiously most of the night.

Debbie Bollinger grabbed her daughter when she saw her and said, "I'm going to nail her feet to the terra firma for a while."

Tammy Moore, whose 14-year-old daughter Savannah was on Flight 237, felt nauseous until she saw her daughter's face.

"Our hearts go out to the people who won't see their families tonight," she said. Savannah said passengers were not told of the plane crash. She thought a celebrity was on board when she saw the TV cameras at the gate.

At a different gate, where another flight from Puerto Vallarta was arriving, Renea Zosel was waiting for her mother and brother.

"Just for a few seconds, the world ended," she said. "When it's close to home, I feel sick for everyone else."

On the Los Angeles leg of that flight, Pedro Orozco said the captain yelled at the passengers and told them not to ask any questions about the crash. "It was really creepy," he said.

Many of Alaska's other flights were delayed, but much of the airport—other than the private grieving room—appeared to be doing business as usual. In one bar, the TV was trained on sports, not on the news.

"It's unfortunate, but it's not going to stop me from flying," said one airport employee. "It's still safer to fly than drive."

P-I reporters Judd Slivka, Candy Hatcher, Tracy Johnson, Heath Foster and Lisa Stiffler contributed to this report.

INTERNET EXERCISES

There are several Web sites with good advice for aspiring feature writers:

Find tips from William E. Blundell, a master of the craft, at **http://www.freep.com/ jobspage/academy/blundell.htm**.

Read AP trainer Barbara King's advice about getting real people into stories at **http://www.freep.com/jobspage/academy/king.htm**.

Leonard Pitts Jr. talks about writing from the heart at **http://www.freep.com/jobspage/academy/pitts.htm**.

Check out Peggy Walsh-Sarnecki's caution against overusing feature leads at **http://www.freep.com/jobspage/academy/anecdote.htm**.

Many straight news stories can be rewritten in a feature-oriented style with a delayed lead. Log onto some hard-news Web sites, find some straight-news news stories and rewrite them. Even if you just turn a hard-news lead into a feature lead, it's good practice.

The major wire services, which make hard-newswriting their stock in trade, are a good place to start:

The Associated Press   **http://wire.ap.org**

Reuters   **http://www.reuters.com**

United Press International   **http://www.upi.com**

BEYOND THE CLASSROOM

1. Interview a professor at your college or an interesting person in your community. Write a profile of that person, using a delayed lead and a descriptive writing style.
2. Cover a hard-news event for your student newspaper, and write it as a straight news story. Then try rewriting it as a feature story with a delayed lead.

Associated Press Style

Note: This is only a very brief summary of some of the main points of AP style. When in doubt, always check your stylebook.

Numerals

One through nine are generally spelled out; 10 and above are generally numbers.

He has five goats, eight dogs, 14 fish and 23 mice.

Exceptions to the general rule include the following: Ages are always numbers:

The boy is 5 years old, the 5-year-old boy, the 80-year-old man.

Percentages are always numbers, but use *percent*, not %:

The business lost 5 percent of its revenue.

Dimensions are always numbers:

She weighs 120 pounds and is 5 feet 6 inches tall.

Times

6 p.m., not *6:00 p.m.*

6 a.m.

6:30 p.m.

8 tonight, not *8 p.m. tonight,* which is redundant.

Months, Dates

January, February, August, September, October, November and December are the only months abbreviated in dates:

Nov. 11, but *April 11 (not Apr. 11)*

Spell out otherwise:

He was born in September.

When referring to events in the past, only give the year if it didn't happen the year in which you are writing:

He visited us on Oct. 15, 2001.

But,

We will visit New York this Sept. 11.

Money

5 cents

50 cents

$5

$5.50

$50

$500

$5,000

$5,000,000

$5 million

$5.5 million

$5 billion

and so on . . .

Addresses

Abbreviate St., Ave., Blvd., etc., if they appear after a numbered address. Spell them out and capitalize when referring to a specific street without an address. Other words used to describe a street—like road, route, etc.—are never abbreviated.

He lives at 123 Main St.

He walked down Main Street.

She lives at 1440 Blackhawk Road.

Job Titles

Capitalize before the name, but not after:

President George W. Bush
George W. Bush, the president of the United States

Punctuation

Place periods and commas inside quotation marks:

"We walked down the street," not *"we walked down the street".*

States and Countries

Spell out the names of all of the states when they stand alone.

He lives in Alaska.

Spell out the United States. Abbreviate it as U.S. only as an adjective before a noun.

We live in the United States.

The U.S. economy is showing a decline.

Abbreviate state names only when used with a city.

They live in Tampa, Fla.

But,

They live in Florida.

These are the abbreviations for the states:

Ala., Ariz., Ark., Calif., Colo., Conn., D.C., Del., Fla., Ga., Ill., Ind., Kan., Ky., La., Md., Mass., Mich., Minn., Mo., Mont., Neb., Nev., N.H., N.J., N.M., N.Y., N.C., N.D., Okla., Ore., Pa., R.I., S.C., S.D., Tenn., Vt., Va., Wash., W. Va., Wis., Wyo.

Alaska, Hawaii, Idaho, Iowa, Maine, Ohio, Utah and Texas are never abbreviated.

Omit the names of states after the largest cities such as New York, Chicago, and Los Angeles. A full list of these cities is in the stylebook.

appendix

B

Math for Reporters

Let's face it—math and reporters often don't mix. Journalists generally get into their profession because they are word people, not numbers people (although there certainly are plenty of exceptions). But like it or not, even reporters need to be able to do basic math, and this applies to nearly every beat. Whether it's the city hall reporter checking the figures in the mayor's budget or the business reporter going over a company's earnings report, the ability to understand basic math is essential. Here, then, is a basic math primer.

Percentages

Percentages are used to help people understand changes in a number or value over time. To calculate a percentage, simply subtract the old value from the new value, then divide that by the old value. Multiply the result by 100. That's the percentage change.

Let's say Centerville had 28 murders last year and 42 this year.

42 − 28 = 14

14 ÷ 28 = 0.5

0.5 × 100 = 50 percent

There was a 50 percent increase in murders in Centerville this year over last year.

Mean

To calculate the mean, simply add up all the values in a set of data and then divide that sum by the number of values in the dataset.

Let's say you are writing about salaries at Centerville City Hall. The mayor makes $80,000; the deputy mayor makes $50,000; the five members of the city council each make $40,000; the city clerk makes $25,000; and the mayor's secretary makes $20,000.

$80,000 + $50,000 + $40,000 + $40,000 + $40,000 + $40,000 + $40,000 + $28,000 + $22,000 = $375,000.

134

$375,000 ÷ 9 = $41,666.

The mean salary at Centerville City Hall is $41,666.

Median

The median represents the average number in a set of values, and is generally more representative than the mean. To calculate the median you simply line up the values you're using, from largest to smallest. The one in the middle is your median.

Let's return to the example of the Centerville City Hall employees.

$80,000

$50,000

$40,000

$40,000

$40,000

$40,000

$40,000

$25,000

$20,000

As you see, the figure in the middle of these values is $40,000. That's the median.

Rate

A rate is a relationship between two numbers. In journalism we often write about crime rates, which are generally the number of crimes in a given city or state for every 100,000 people. Rates are usually more meaningful than raw numbers in these cases, because the population is factored into the equation. For example, New York City had 672 murders in 2001, according to the FBI's Uniform Crime Reports, while Memphis, Tenn., had 175. At first glance, it would seem like Memphis is a much safer city, right?

But New York City, the nation's largest metropolis, has 9.3 million inhabitants, while Memphis has 1.1 million. So while New York City's murder *rate* is 7.2 murders per 100,000 people, Memphis' is actually higher—15.3 murders per 100,000 people. New Yorkers could easily argue that theirs is the safer city.

To calculate the rate, divide the number of murders by the total population of the city, then multiply the result by 100,000. That gives you the rate per 100,000 people. Here's the calculation for New York:

$672 ÷ 9,300,000 = .00007226 × 100,000 = 7.2

Math Quiz

1. Centerville had 563 armed robberies last year and 608 this year. Calculate the percentage change.
2. Centerville's population was 153,540 five years ago. It's now 166,432. Calculate the percentage change.
3. Al's Deli employs five people. Here are their salaries:
   Al, the owner: $58,000
   Janet, the bookkeeper: $42,000
   Fred, the sandwich maker: $28,000
   Lilith, the cashier: $22,000
   Joe, the janitor: $18,000
   Calculate the mean and the median salary at Al's Deli.

4. Albuquerque, N.M., has a population of 716,696. It had 44 murders in 2001. Calculate the rate per 100,000 inhabitants.
5. Trenton, N.J., has 353,682 inhabitants. It had 939 robberies in 2001. Calculate the rate per 100,000 inhabitants.

C

Web Resources

Journalism Schools

American University School of Communication
http://www.soc.american.edu/

Arizona State University–Walter Cronkite School of Journalism and Telecommunication
http://www.asu.edu/cronkite/

Ball State University Department of Journalism
http://www.bsu.edu/journalism/

Boston University College of Communication
http://www.bu.edu/com/communication.html

Bowling Green State University Department of Telecommunications
http://www.bgsu.edu/Departments/tcom/

Bradley University College of Communications and Fine Arts
http://www.bradley.edu/academics/cfa/cfa.html

Brigham Young University College of Fine Arts and Communications
http://www.byu.edu/cfac/departments/

Brown University Department of Modern Culture and Media
http://www.brown.edu/Departments/MCM/

California State University at Chico Department of Journalism
http://www.csuchico.edu/jour/

Columbia University Graduate School of Journalism
http://www.jrn.columbia.edu/

Eastern Illinois University Journalism Department
http://www.eiu.edu/~journal/

Florida International University School of Journalism and Mass Communication
http://www.fiu.edu/~journal/

George Washington University School of Communications
http://www.gwu.edu/~commgwu/

Hamline University Department of Communication Arts
http://www.hamline.edu/depts/commdept/

Harvard University, Joan Shorenstein Barone Center on the Press, Politics & Public Policy
http://ksgwww.harvard.edu/shorenstein/

Indiana University School of Journalism
http://journalism.indiana.edu/

Kansas State University, The A. Q. Miller School of Journalism and Mass Communications
http://www.jmc.ksu.edu/

Kent State University School of Journalism and Mass Communication
http://www.jmc.kent.edu/

Lehigh University Department of Journalism and Communication
http://www.lehigh.edu/injrl/public/www-data/injrl.html

Louisiana State University, The Manship School of Mass Communication
http://www.manship.lsu.edu/

Michigan State University School of Journalism
http://jrn.msu.edu/programs/index.html

New York University Department of Journalism and Mass Communication
http://journalweb.journalism.fas.nyu.edu/

Northwestern University, The Medill School of Journalism
http://www.medill.northwestern.edu/

Ohio University, E. W. Scripps School of Journalism
http://scrippsjschool.org/

Rutgers, State University of New Jersey School of Communication
http://www.scils.rutgers.edu/

San Francisco State University Department of Journalism
http://www.journalism.sfsu.edu

San Jose State University School of Journalism & Mass Communications
http://www.jmc.sjsu.edu/index.html

Southampton College Department of Communication Arts
http://www.southampton.liunet.edu/academic/courses/u_comm.htm

Southern Illinois University at Carbondale, School of Journalism
http://www.siu.edu/departments/journal/

Syracuse University, Newhouse School of Public Communication
http://newhouse.syr.edu/

Temple University School of Journalism
http://www.temple.edu/jpra/

University of Arizona School of Journalism
http://journalism.arizona.edu/

University of California at Berkeley Graduate School of Journalism
http://www.journalism.berkeley.edu/

University of Dayton, Department of Communication
http://artssciences.udayton.edu/communication/

University of Florida College of Journalism and Communications
http://www.jou.ufl.edu/

University of Georgia, Henry W. Grady College of Journalism and Mass Communication
http://www.grady.uga.edu/

University of Hawaii at Manoa Department of Communication
http://www2.soc.hawaii.edu/css/com/

University of Illinois College of Communications
http://www.uiuc.edu/providers/comm/

University of Iowa School of Journalism and Mass Communication
http://www.uiowa.edu/~journal/index.html

University of Kansas, William Allen White School of Journalism and Mass Communications
http://www.cc.ukans.edu/~jschool/

University of Maine Department of Communications and Journalism
http://www.ume.maine.edu/"coj/depthomp.htm/

University of Maryland at College Park College of Journalism
http://www.journalism.umd.edu/

University of Minnesota Department of Journalism
http://www1.umn.edu/commpub/c_cla/cla_44.html

University of Missouri at Columbia School of Journalism
http://www.journalism.missouri.edu/

University of Nevada at Reno, Reynolds School of Journalism
http://www.unr.edu/journalism/

University of North Carolina at Chapel Hill School of Journalism and Mass Communication
http://www.ibiblio.org/jomc/

University of Oklahoma Gaylord College of Journalism and Mass Communication
http://jmc.ou.edu//

University of Oregon School of Journalism and Communications
http://jcomm.uoregon.edu/

University of Pennsylvania, Annenberg School for Communication
http://jcomm.uoregon.edu/

University of South Carolina College of Journalism and Mass Communication
http://www.jour.sc.edu/

University of Southern California, Annenberg School of Communication
http://ascweb.usc.edu/home.php

University of Texas at Austin College of Communication
http://communication.utexas.edu/

University of Wisconsin at Madison School of Journalism and Communications
http://www.journalism.wisc.edu/

University of Wisconsin-Milwaukee, Department of Mass Communications
http://www.uwm.edu/Dept/JMC/

University of Wisconsin at River Falls Department of Journalism
http://www.uwrf.edu/journalism/welcome.html

Utah State University Department of Communication
http://www.usu.edu/communic/

Vanderbilt University Department of Communication Studies and Theater
http://www.vanderbilt.edu/AnS/Comm/

Western Michigan University Department of Communication
http://www.wmich.edu/communication/

Washington University Department of Journalism
http://www.ac.wwu.edu/~journal/

Journalism Organizations

Committee to Protect Journalists
http://www.cpj.org/

Reporters Committee for Freedom of the Press
http://www.rcfp.org/

The Newspaper Guild
http://newsguild.org/

Student Press Law Center
http://www.splc.org/

College Media Advisers
http://www.collegemedia.org/

Associated Collegiate Press
http://www.studentpress.org/acp/

Columbia Scholastic Press Association
http://www.columbia.edu/cu/cspa/

The Freedom Forum
http://www.freedomforum.org/

The Poynter Institute
http://www.poynter.org/

The Pulitzer Prizes
http://www.pulitzer.org/

Society of Professional Journalists
http://www.spj.org/

Society of Environmental Journalists
http://www.sej.org/

Investigative Reporters and Editors
http://www.ire.org/

National Association of Black Journalists
http://www.nabj.org/

National Association of Hispanic Journalists
http://www.nahj.org/

Asian American Journalists Association
http://www.aaja.org/

International Freedom of Expression Exchange
http://www.ifex.org/

National Press Club
http://www.nationalpressclub/.org/

Journalism Publications and Web Sites

American Journalism Review
http://www.ajr.org/

Columbia Journalism Review
http://www.cjr.org/

Editor and Publisher
http://www.mediainfo.com/editorandpublisher/index.jsp

Jim Romenesko's Media News
http://www.poynter.org/column.asp?id=45

Newswatch
http://www.newswatch.org/index.html

I Want Media
http://iwantmedia.com/

Inside.com
http://www.inside.com/

Media Channel
http://www.mediachannel.org/

Online NewsHour Media Watch
http://www.pbs.org/newshour/media/

Online Journalism Review
http://www.ojr.org/ojr/page_one/index.php

Journalism Jobs

Job Hunting Tips from the Detroit Free Press
http://www.freep.com/jobspage/toolkit/index.htm

Editor and Publisher Magazine classifieds
http://www.mediainfo.com/editorandpublisher/classifieds/index.jsp

JournalismJobs.com
http://www.journalismjobs.com/

Newsjobs.net
http://www.newsjobs.net/Jobs/default.asp

Newsjobs.com
http://www.newsjobs.com/

Knight-Ridder Newspapers
http://www.kri.com/

Gannett Newspapers
http://www.gannett.com/

Journalism Job Bank
http://www.journalism.berkeley.edu/jobs/

Newslink Joblink
http://newslink.org/joblink/

Copy Editing Jobs
http://www.copyeditor.com/default.asp?id=3

TV News Jobs
http://tvnewz.com/

Dow Jones Jobs
http://www.dowjones.com/careers/djc_srch.htm

TV Jobs
http://www.tvjobs.com/jbcenter.htm

Glossary of Journalism Terms

AP Style   A set format for writing things such as dates, dollar amounts, titles, addresses and the like in news stories.

Assignment Editor   An editor who deals directly with reporters in assigning stories and coordinating news coverage, as opposed to a *copy editor*. Assignment editors are usually responsible for specific sections of the newspaper, such as city news, sports or features.

Associated Press   The world's oldest and largest news service. Sometimes referred to as a wire service, the AP distributes news stories to newspapers and broadcast outlets around the world.

Attribution   Telling the reader where the information in a news story comes from, whether from official sources, individuals the reporter has interviewed, or the reporter's own observations.

Balance   Giving all sides of an issue being covered in a news story equal time and treatment. For instance, the reporter covering a city council meeting at which tax increases are being discussed should interview both proponents and opponents of the proposal.

Beat   The specific area of news a reporter covers. Typical beats include police, fire, the courts, etc.

Bureau   A newspaper office located at some distance from the paper's main office. The New York Times, for instance, is headquartered in Manhattan but has news bureaus around the world.

Byline   The name of the reporter who wrote the story.

Clip   A published writing sample. It's important to have these when applying for reporting jobs.

Copy   News writing.

Copy editor   An editor who edits news stories primarily for grammar, punctuation and AP style. Copy editors usually write headlines for stories, but they typically don't deal directly with reporters in the way an *assignment editor* does.

Dateline   The city from which a story originates.

Deadline   The time when news stories must be done in order to be published in the next day's newspaper.

Delayed lead, or feature lead   A lead used in *features*. Instead of summarizing the main points in the first paragraph, the delayed lead leads the reader into the story for several paragraphs, using description or an anecdote to begin telling the reader what the story is about. The story is then summarized in the *nut graph*.

Editorial   An opinion column that usually runs on the editorial page.

Enterprise reporting   Stories developed from the reporter's own ideas, observation and investigation, as opposed to coverage of breaking news events.

Feature   A story that tends to emphasize human-interest elements more than a straight hard-news story. Feature stories tend to emphasize description, mood and atmosphere than hard-news stories.

Five W's and H   This refers to who, what, where, when, why and how, the elements a reporter tries to incorporate into the lead of a news story.

Hard-news story   A story written in classic inverted pyramid form as opposed to the way a feature is written.

Inverted pyramid   The classic model for news writing, it means that the most important, or heaviest news, should come right at the start of the news story, in the lead. Less important, or lighter news, should come later in the story, near the bottom.

Lead   The first paragraph in a hard-news story. It should summarize the main points of the story but not get bogged down in small details. Generally, it should be no more than 35 words.

Mainbar   On big stories, this term refers to the main news story about the event, as opposed to the *sidebar*.

News digest   A list of all the stories due to appear in the next day's paper. Also called the news budget, this list by used by editors for organizational purposes.

News hole   The amount of space available in the paper for news stories after advertisements have been placed on the pages.

News meeting   A daily meeting at which editors decide which stories will run in the next day's paper, and where those stories will be placed.

Nut graph   The paragraph in a feature story that acts as the lead by explaining what the story is about.

Obituary   Also called an obit; a story about someone who has died.

Objectivity   The idea that hard-news stories should not take a position or editorialize on the topic or event being covered, but instead should be written in a detached, neutral tone.

Sidebar   A story focusing on one particular angle of an event, as opposed to the *mainbar*. Sidebars are often used on very big breaking news stories in conjunction with the mainbar.

SVO   Subject-verb-object. This is writing in the active voice: *She hit the ball*. The active voice is generally preferred in newswriting because it is shorter and more vivid, as opposed to the passive voice: *The ball was hit by her*.

Index

Credits

Page **1**, Courtesy of Tony Rogers; **10**, Courtesy of Tony Rogers; **18**, Photo courtesy of the Bucks County Courier Times; **21**, Reprinted courtesy of Court TV's thesmokinggun.com; **23**, Reprinted courtesy of Court TV's thesmokinggun.com; **25**, Reprinted courtesy of Court TV's thesmokinggun.com; **28**, Reprinted courtesy of Court TV's thesmokinggun.com; **29**, Reprinted courtesy of Court TV's thesmokinggun.com; **30**, Reprinted courtesy of Court TV's thesmokinggun.com; **32**, Courtesy of Mike Claffey; **35**, Photo courtesy of the Bucks County Courier Times; **44**, Courtesy of Darrell Smith; **48**, Photo courtesy of the Bucks County Courier Times; **51**, Photo courtesy of the Bucks County Courier Times; **54**, Courtesy of the National Oceanic and Atmospheric Administration; **58**, Courtesy of Stephen Manning; **62**, Photo courtesy of the Bucks County Courier Times; **69**, Courtesy of Jena Heath; **74**, Photo courtesy of the Bucks County Courier Times; **80**, Courtesy of Ross Markman; **84**, Photo courtesy of the Bucks County Courier Times; **88**, Courtesy of Robb Luehr; **92**, Photo courtesy of the Bucks County Courier Times; **98**, Photo courtesy of Getahn Ward; **101**, Photo courtesy of the Bucks County Courier Times; **106**, Courtesy of Jere Hester; **111**, Photo courtesy of the Bucks County Courier Times; **117**, Courtesy of Daniel Q. Haney; **121**, Photo courtesy of the Bucks County Courier Times; **127**, Courtesy of Vanessa Ho.